ENLIGHTENMENT

ENLIGHTENMENT

~ The Manual ~

David A. Scott

ISBN (softcover): 978-1-0688261-0-8
ISBN (Ebook): 978-1-0688261-1-5

First Edition
Cover artwork by Joe Alrutz at MaxsCoolShirts
Printed and bound in the United States of America

Table of Contents

We are born into a Cosmic Predicament….

> Marooned on an island in a sea of stars,
> with no good answers to the most pressing
> questions….

> > What is going on?
> > How do I make sense of this?
> > What does it all mean?
> > Who am I?
> > Why?

> > Why *me*?

THEORY

Chapter 1

"They say in Zen, when you attain *satori*, nothing is left you at that moment but to have a good laugh."
~ Alan Watts, "Out of Your Mind"

The Moment of Self-Realization (and the Cosmic Joke)

As soon as we wake up, the lights go on in the inner theatre, the curtain goes up, and the drama begins again. Spectacular thoughts!   Riveting sensations!   Gut-wrenching feelings!   Implacable cravings!   Erotic tableaux! Love! Rejection! Spine-tingling revelations! Jealousy! Despair! Existential crises! Orgasms! The Dark Night of the Soul! The White Light!

Insight.

I'm walking by the liquor store lost in thought and suddenly—it hits me! And I'm literally stopped in my tracks. I have slipped into a rare but familiar state of mind that grips me with awe, fascination— dumbfoundedness.

In Normal Waking Reality we are usually absorbed by the drama playing out in our heads. We are lost in thought, overwhelmed by an emotion, propelled by a desire, and so on. We don't notice the absorption in the same way that a fish does not notice the stream it swims in. To notice the stream, the fish would have to "rise above" (or breach) it, or the water would have to slowly evaporate. In our own case, our absorptions or automatic behaviors become noticeable when we similarly rise above them or "catch ourselves in the act."

This internal "view from above" is called the Meta-View, and as we shall see, it is a critical shift in our consciousness which can turn the mind into a dynamic playground as well as a source of invaluable insights.

Now let's turn our attention to our sense of self. This is the elemental sense of self we wake up to every morning that tells us it's the same "me" that fell asleep the night before. This is not the descriptive extended self that contains our history, temperament, ambitions, and so on. Most critically for our purposes here, the extended self also contains what we identify with, such as gender, race, nationality, political leanings, and the rest. It's the self we refer to when asked, "Who are you?" In sum, the extended self encompasses everything *about* us; the core sense of self is just that: the *sense* of familiar continuity that attends every element in our stream of consciousness. That's how we know these are *my* feelings, *my* thoughts, and so on. Every moment of conscious awareness is twofold: a static agent absorbed in a dynamic story. This arrangement predisposes greater interest in the story than the agent. It is analogous to watching a movie and being so absorbed in the action that we don't notice the presence of the camera in the scene. In the same way we don't give our core sense of self much thought *as an item* in the inner theatre.

Now notice what has just happened.

The core sense of self is a wholly subjective entity. As the philosophers characterize it, it has a 1st Person ontology (as opposed to a 3rd Person ontology like any object in the external world). It is (merely) a brain process. As soon as we begin to think about our core sense of self or ascribe qualities to it, we have made it into at least an *object* of thought. And if you are now thinking about your own sense of self, you have shifted into the Meta-View. And you may well have, without intending to, formed an image of it, possibly in color. If that is so, then you have experienced first-hand how the mind *reifies* (constructs, makes up) elements in its worldview (more in Chapter 6).

Now what happens when you remain aware of your *sense* of self at the same time you think about it as an object? And then (up another level) you visualize it as an object within space and time?

This was my Moment in front of the liquor store. I suddenly noticed my sense of *me-ness* and began to marvel about it. I recognized that what was looking through my eyes was a unique entity that had appeared out of nowhere nearly 14 billion years after the Big Bang! How did "me" come to be? And most important of all: Why? The lack of any satisfying answers to these questions is at the heart of our Cosmic Predicament. It didn't and doesn't make any sense.

Take a moment and contemplate *your* experience of your sense of self in space and time. What comes up?

I call this state the Moment of Cosmic Self-Realization—or simply the Moment.

I've had these Moments from a very young age. I remember trying to explain it to my father one time under the weeping willow tree in the backyard. I think I was about eight.

"I'm in me," I tried, "and you're in you...."

I had the feeling he understood. He murmured, "Mm-hmm" but was unable to contribute anything more to what I was trying to say.

I grew up assuming that everyone else had these Moments, but when I asked around, most people seemed not to understand what I was talking about. Blank stares, change of subject, shaking heads. To be sure, the Moment is a step out of ordinary awareness. Normal Waking Reality (NWR) and the Moment are two separate perspectives or involvements with the world. NWR has more demands and attractions than our attention span can contain. Daily life is occupied with plans, problems, regrets, fears, cravings, working, studying, watching TV, caring for the kids, driving, making love, opinions on UFOs, and so on. There's precious little time for either navel- or star-gazing. Our NWR conversations do, of course, include the "mystery of life," but talking about it is not the same as being steeped in its phenomenology. Going there may seem to be quirky, freaky or a complete waste of time, but I was nonetheless surprised by the lack of engagement in what, in my mind, is the Big Lebowski.

How many people have had these Moments and written about them? I have searched far and wide for accounts of the Moment and so far, have found only a handful.

This one is from the philosopher, Thomas Nagel, who is perhaps best known for his essay, "What Is it Like to Be a Bat?"

> It isn't easy to absorb the fact that I am contained in the world at all. It seems outlandish that the centerless universe, in all its spatiotemporal immensity, should have produced me, of all people.... There was no such thing as me for ages, but with the formation of a particular physical organism at a particular place and time, suddenly there *is* me, for as long as the organism survives. In the objective flow of the

> cosmos this subjectively (to me!) stupendous event produces hardly a ripple. How can the existence of one member of one species have this remarkable consequence?[1]

All irony hinges on the following fact: the mental apparatus responsible for "making sense of it all" is incapable of making sense of itself.

The Moment is a place in my mind. It is one of several I have discovered that fall within the category of altered states. Altered states lie beyond the realm of Normal Waking Reality. NWR is comprised of those states that maintain the status quo. If I didn't have these places to go to, life would be comparatively dull. The inward exploration of the mind's landscape, its highs and lows, twists and turns, is what I live for. Stretch it out of all proportion. Strap it, snap it, spank it. Torture it a little. Take it to the extremes (if only, as the Buddhists say, to find the middle ground). Blast it to blissed out peaks, smear it out and drop to the cellar of despair and hopelessness. Turn it in on itself to find the Void. Investigate its patterns. Refine it in the light of common sense. Challenge its views, ethics and values. Perhaps I can see how it all fits together and discover my true self—unfettered and unformatted by the NWR of the cultural surround.

What is "altered" in altered states is the normal state. They are a latent potentiality within NWR. All they require is a certain stimulus within a certain setting. Drugs, alcohol, deep breathing, meditation, dreaming, orgasm, deep thinking, as well as recombining the normal elements of consciousness such as thoughts, feelings, and mental focus—these are all gateways to esoteric realms.

Of what use is the Moment? If it reminds us of our Cosmic Predicament and offers no answers to the really important questions, why would it be meaningful or even worthy of attention? I think for a few very good reasons.

1. The Moment highlights the distinction between the absorbed state and the Meta-View

Our normal state is to be preoccupied with our stream of mental content—thoughts, feelings, etc.—which psychologists describe as a state of "Automaticity." We might call it being on auto-pilot. It is thought that we spend about 95% of our waking hours there. (Automaticity will be explored further in later chapters.) Shifting to the Meta-View places the automatic stream in relief. We become aware of it as a conscious state (like a fish out of water), can observe it stream along from a remote POV, and then change the stream's direction. Perhaps most significantly, we can use the Meta-View to change some of our programmed responses to the world.

2. The Moment highlights the distinction between our core sense of self and our extended self.

The extended self is the repository of our self-attributions, most notably for our purposes here, what we identify with. These include gender, sexual orientation, race, religion, nationality, political affiliation, and so on, all of which are essentially culturally defined, certainly culturally influenced. The extended self serves to objectify who we are in our own eyes and in the eyes of others. Identifying with a particular group satisfies our need for belonging, but at the same time creates antagonistic divisions. Research has shown that randomly dividing subjects into groups labelled only A and B was "enough to trigger discriminatory behavior" between them.[2] It would seem that tribalism is woven into our DNA. From very old times, being a member of a sizable clan probably had survival value well beyond being alone or even a member of a much smaller group. So we may be disposed to belong to a group and view it as superior to other groups. That is, until we begin to identify with something more elemental and unifying.

Such as our core sense of self. It is the naked, raw, unattributed identity of who we are. And here in this rarefied experience, we are all the same. We are all united in the same unfathomable mystery. We are all unwitting participants in the Great Cosmic Predicament (otherwise known as the Divine Comedy).

The self in the Moment transcends every attributed group identity that we subscribe to. Gender, race, religion, and the rest, are all secondary artefacts that we subscribe to in various ways.

Where we do not recognize the similarities among people at the deepest level, we are left only with the superficial differences that divide us. Now imagine if we identified with the self in the Moment and viewed all the secondary identifiers in others as flavors or hues in a playful pageantry. The self in the Moment could conceivably be the basis for a universal religion. And all the major conflicts would simply end. The experience of the Moment is the tide that washes away all dominions.

3. The Moment is a Rorschach for how we feel about it.

One could easily react to the Moment with surprise, uncanniness (Nagel), anger, resentment—or fear. This is how the French scientist and mystic, Blaise Pascal, expressed his experience of the Moment, in the 17th Century:

> When I consider the brief span of my life,
> swallowed up in the eternity before and
> behind it, the small space that I fill, or even
> see, engulfed in the infinite immensity of
> spaces which I know not, and which know

not me, I am afraid, and wonder to see myself here rather than there; for there is no reason why I should be here rather than there, now rather than then. Who has set me here? By whose order and arrangement have this place and this time been allotted to me? The eternal silence of these infinite spaces frightens me.[3]

In the early days the Moment gave me a certain eerie feeling similar to Nagel's. And then as I got used to it, it lessened in intensity. It became somewhat normalized. And then I saw the humor in it all. I "got" the Great Cosmic Joke.

To get your own Moment, focus on your sense of self, its continuity from moment to moment, the knowing that it's *you*; and now contemplate the fact that there is no good explanation for it and never will be. We are all flukes, twists of fate. That's just the way it is. That is the Cosmic Predicament. How do you react to that? You could be extremely disturbed by it—or you could throw your head back in raucous gut-splitting laughter. It is my recollection that Alan Watts started every morning by looking in a mirror and laughing as hard as he could. You can find a sound track of him laughing on the Web. It is worth hearing.

What is the joke? The alchemy of a joke is in its delivery, not its explanation, and I think everyone will get the joke in their own way. Perhaps it is the sudden revelation that who you thought you were all this time (your ego) is mostly a construction, a fantasy, a story you tell yourself. Perhaps the veil on human pretense, pomposity, and self-importance suddenly dropped away. Or you saw that an uncertainty principle is woven into all the existential questions. I think the essence of the joke is seeing that what you took so seriously—isn't.

I begin with the Moment because it gives you an experience of your sense of self in the raw. This is the one thing about you that does not change. It carries your continuity. An hour from now or years from now, you will still be able to access the same sense of self. It is entirely phenomenological, that is, it does not translate into a tangible objective thing that can be placed on a table for further analysis. It is a wholly subjective experience. It has no solid foundation. And yet it is the centerpiece in the catalogue of what goes on inside our heads. And yet again, the concerted experience of the self at this level is a rarity among human beings. We get stuck in the stuff upstairs, our extended selves, essentially who we think we are. Who we think we *really* are. And that's where the conflict begins. At the level of the Moment, the self is merely this tender sense of a continuous entity known as "me"—and nothing else. There is no complexity here, no cognitive dissonance, no flaw. These are all generated from "above" with a big helping hand from our thinking processes.

Your sense of self in the Moment is a spiritual, holy moment; embrace it with solemnity (once the laughter dies down).

Chapter 2

"That man can interrogate as well as observe nature,
was a lesson slowly learned in his evolution."
~ Sir William Osler, "Aphorisms"

Lucid Focusing

One morning, I was walking home in the cold taking note of its effects on my body. The sensation chilled my arms, legs and face. It was also attended by a visual aspect at each place, a white-wide glow that thickened toward the middle and fringed out at the edges. Then I noticed something else in the mix. The thought occurred that if I had just been sprung from a meat freezer, just before going unconscious, the cold of this winter afternoon would not be as disagreeable as it was. It might in fact be relatively warm. But since that was not the case, I just felt cold and didn't much like it. That was the something else—not liking it. Attached to the cold at each spot was a clench of resistance that gathered in my consciousness.

The feeling of resistance produced an increased tension in my muscles at the cold points. I was literally scrunched up against the cold. I told myself to "relax" and just accept the cold for what it was. The tension subsided, my shoulders dropped, and the resistance dissolved. The sensation of coldness remained as intense, but my overall reaction to the cold was much better. Something had changed.

In Normal Waking Reality, I am carried along by a stream of cause and effect. One thing leads to another. Thoughts spring up, images flash on, feelings well up and cravings take hold, further provoking each other in an ever-changing chain of intrigue. I refer to this as the absorbed state. But sometimes I catch myself in the act. When this happens, there is a separation between the stream and the agent at the center—the "I." I am now observing the stream of thoughts, feelings, and so on. I have moved out of the absorbed state into what is known as meta-conscious awareness or the Meta-View.

In this special configuration in the mental theatre, the stream moves from a subjective state to an objective one since I am no longer *in* the stream, but observing it. What I noticed was that when I focused on a negative feeling, consciously accepted it, and stopped thinking, the feeling dissolved. I tried it on loneliness and boredom which had been my only recent companions, especially at night. I sat with the feelings, focusing on them, visualizing them in my body, for about two hours—and they eventually vanished! Lucid dreaming gave me the idea to call this mental process Lucid Focusing. They both aim at changing plotlines.

The idea that I could change what goes on inside my mind, especially the painful stuff, posed many questions. How far can I take this idea? How far will my own mind allow me to tinker with it? Can I actually streamline its operation toward a self-actualized, confident and fulfilled human being? Is it possible to be free of conflict, anxiety, feelings of rejection, unhealthy cravings, and the big four: anger, fear, shame and guilt? Can I make life more pleasurable from the inside? Is there a sublime arrangement approximating "the answer"? Can I just make some sort of peace with this existence?

During the Sixties, the concept of enlightenment was in the wind. Buddhism, Hinduism and LSD had collided in the Western World, and testimonials about peak states of consciousness from both sides of the aisle suggested that the two paths led to the same place. An anecdote from Baba Ram Dass (Timothy Leary's protégé) cemented the deal. When he was in India, Ram Dass gave an Indian holy man three tabs of acid, amounting to 915 micrograms, a very large dose. Yet the drug seemed to have no effect. Apparently the holy man was already there.

Then I experienced it myself on a tab of acid in a rural house north of Montreal. I describe the experience in the next chapter. For now I'll just say that it was mind-blowing.

Many questions arise. Was my experience true enlightenment? Was Ram Dass's holy man in the state of enlightenment or in a state somewhat "below"? But the most intriguing question for me was, if the state of enlightenment is a latent feature of the psyche, nudgeable either by an extended mental discipline or in a flash with a drug, was there a Middle Way, a process or exercise that could produce the enlightened state in a relatively short period of time and without the use of drugs?

This question occurred to me somewhat late in life. By that time, I had trekked the conscious-raising trail through NLP, est, Context, breath work, Transcendental Meditation, and rolfing, and spent eight months roaming around India looking for answers. Each occasioned some insight and noticeable change in my consciousness, but, as they say, something was still missing.

So I determined to figure it out for myself—from the inside. In a sort of Cartesian analysis, I catalogued all the different actors in the inner theatre of my mind. René Descartes bequeathed to us the phrase, "I think; therefore I am" at the end of his quest to see if there was anything real inside his head. The mind can be a dynamic place. So many different processes all occurring in the same mental space. It is not easy to separate one from the other, not only because the inward gaze required for the operation affects what goes on there. Descartes decided that the one thing that could not be dismissed was his thinking. My quest was different. I wanted to see how the different elements in the inner theatre related to each other and see if they could be rearranged to operate more in my self-interest.

And they can. I found out how to raise my general mood, dissolve (most of) my shame, rid myself of triggers, become more spontaneous, have clearer thoughts, and actually come to care about myself. I dumped some very old and gnarly baggage.

It's not that difficult to clear your mind of almost all of the junk in there. It doesn't take a long period of meditation or a potent substance. You are likely to see some results very quickly.

In what follows, I will reveal all my research on enlightenment, offer a brief soliloquy on how much pain we're all in, an extensive exploration of the "self," our self-evaluations, shame, a catalogue of the inner theatre, and several exercises to move you along the path to your own enlightenment.

Chapter 3

"The true value of a human being is determined primarily by the measure and the sense in which he has attained liberation from the self".
~ Albert Einstein, *The World as I See It.*

Enlightenment

What is it really?

The word "enlightenment" suggests a peak in consciousness, a state of illumination, a revelation of deep hidden truths. It suggests a baptism in a burst of light and epiphanic feelings. The following is how the Indian sage, Muktananda, described his experience of samadhi.

> The Light pervaded everywhere in the form of the universe. I saw the earth being born and expanding the Light of Consciousness, just as one can see smoke rising from a fire. I could actually see the world within this conscious Light, and the Light within the world, like threads in a piece of cloth, and cloth in the threads.... I could see this radiance of Consciousness, resplendent and

utterly beautiful, silently pulsing as supreme ecstasy within me, outside me, above me, below me.... In this condition the phenomenal world vanished and I saw only pure radiance.[4]

Latent within our psyches is an experience of profound significance, both to the one experiencing it and to the scientific and philosophical discourses about the mind. Not only is the peak experience earthshaking, it also seems to produce changes in one's perspective and behavior. It is cathartic.

What Hindus call samadhi, Buddhists call nirvana. The epiphanic feelings appear to be similar, but the respective revelations are completely different. In Hinduism, the experience is interpreted to be the merging of the human soul (Atman) with the cosmic consciousness (Brahman). In Buddhism, the peak state reveals that the concept of a permanent self or soul is an *illusion* which lies at the heart of human suffering. Soullessness (anatta) or non-self is one of the three fundamental "marks of existence" (otherwise called "characteristics" and sometimes pillars). This is true for all Buddhist variations, Theravada, Mahayana, Chan, Zen, and so on. The notion of a cosmic consciousness does not figure at all in the religion, so the Buddhist interpretation of the peak experience is fundamentally at odds with Hinduism and all its mystical derivations.[5]

What should we make of two fundamentally different interpretations of the same state of consciousness?

James Austin is a neuroscientist, a Zen practitioner, and the author of the very important book, *Zen and the Brain*. The book examines what happens in both the mind and the brain as the meditator moves through the various levels leading to one-pointedness of mind and eventually, nirvana. I mention both mind and brain, because Austin fleshes out the changes within consciousness (what the meditator experiences) and within the circuitry of the meditator's brain. The physiology isn't important for our purposes here. The intrigue and its significance lie within consciousness. The top end of the meditative arc (nirvana) is characterized by a total shutdown of the cognitive faculties including the sense of self, perception, and bodily awareness (proprioception). What about feeling? Austin says that during nirvana it is simply "inexpressible."[6]

The following is my personal account of reaching the peak under the influence of LSD:

The tab of acid was tagged Berkeley Sunshine, 700 micrograms, split with a friend. Night had fallen and there was a slight drizzle. The acid was already playing havoc with my mind. Everything in my internal map of the world was dividing into categories at lightning speed: trees and flowers into "flora," Earth and Saturn into "planets." Eventually, everything reduced to twelve categories arranged around a clock face. Then there were eight, then four, then only two—pleasure and pain. By this time I had walked into a graveyard and I was standing by a gravestone. In a flash, pain merged with pleasure. The feeling was exactly that: pleasure fused with pain, but the combination instantaneously morphed into something I had never felt before, something mind blowing in its intensity. But only for a very brief moment before my consciousness flashed out in an ecstatic white light. I became the universe, blown out in all directions, expanding into the furthest reaches of space.

Austin explains how during meditation it can seem like one's consciousness expands to the extent that it embraces the cosmos. It is somewhat complex but it has to do with the way we map our spatial coordinates. Our spatial mapping is an internal program (which Austin calls "unconscious circumspatial awareness") that, for instance, tells us how we can get back to the car we just parked. However, during meditation, the space program may become "overactive": "[T]he veil parts, and our subliminal domain of space opens up. Only then—fully conscious at the time—do we discover this vast spatial capacity, and look out into the remarkable theater it has been able to conceive."[7] Austin refers to the apparent merge with the universe as "ambient vision." And he wants to emphasize that "ambient vision is an illusion, a global representation which an overactive brain elaborates under rare circumstances."[8]

The disparity between Hinduism and Buddhism illustrates a critical aspect of our mental experience. The cognitive part is somewhat aloof from everything else going on. If it is shut off at the point of nirvana, it switches back on as soon as the state of nirvana begins to subside. Immediately it attempts to construe and describe what has just happened. When you think about it, arriving at any credible description seems presumptuous simply because there is precious little left "in" the experience to describe. There is some indescribable feeling, perhaps a sense of an expanding void, but little else. There is zero evidence of anything going on outside of the phenomenological realm (other than neural firing). That is, there is no evidence of anything expanding in a three-dimensional, objective sense. All the evidence is "mental" (or phenomenological)—which means that any explanation suggesting objective content is nothing but reification. (Reification will be explored more fully in Chapter 6.) However, it is the job of cognition to come up with some sort of explanation to make sense of it all. Once that is done, the explanation becomes the dogma that explains what happens to everyone else down the line. The Hindu dogma justifies the idea of a cosmic consciousness and the mind's ability to merge with it, when the dogma could conceivably be based on a misperception, an illusion or a hallucination. That would seem to sum up the essence of most, if not all, religious dogmas.

Buddhism is different in that its dogma about nirvana is a *decon*struction rather than a *con*struction. The Buddhist explanation for nirvana deconstructs the reified self (and the soul) that occurs intuitively from naïve perception (the way it seems). In this wise, it is akin to the discovery of the heliocentric solar system (deconstructing the geocentric model), continental drift, and quantum physics. Intuition without corroborating evidence is simply not reliable.

What the Hindu and Buddhist perspectives do share is that the peak experience is an "ultimate" state of mind. So far as we know, there is no level beyond nirvana which, although a product of meditation, is so overwhelming that the cognitive faculties necessary to meditation (such as volition) are simply eclipsed.

Perhaps this is the reason why the peak state eventually subsides. And thankfully so. We can't live out our lives up there. Driving a car, for instance, is impossible at the peak. However, the practice of meditation does, in time, produce an apparently permanent mental state. But it is not the flash of extinguishment in nirvana. The Stage of Ongoing Enlightened Traits (or OET), as Austin calls it, seats itself without fanfare. At some point, consciousness achieves true equanimity, simplicity, and stability, selfless compassion, and a permanent detachment from cravings and aversions.[9] The state of mind persists because brain circuits have changed. We might say that there are two modes of enlightenment, where one is the point and one is the wave.

The "Ongoing" stage (the wave) has extraordinary and provocative implications. It means that woven into the circuitry of the brain is a potential state of saintliness. It means that selfless compassion is not merely a moral precept; it can be an authentic personal orientation. There is a huge difference between how one *should* behave, implying an internal struggle between the "good" and self-interest, and being *of a mind* to be kind to others without even thinking about it. The Golden Rule is meant to keep us focused on the good, but the ongoing spiritual mind needs no moral suasion. That *this* mind is available to us through essentially a specialized self-conditioning of one's consciousness is earthshaking. The idea arises: it's been there all along.

It just has to be nurtured or tapped into. Admittedly, the route to the abiding enlightened mind is not easy. According to Austin, the "Ongoing" state is achieved only after several attainments of nirvana.

So: if the peak is of very short duration and the wave very difficult to obtain, what is there left to crow about?

Chapter 4

"I met in the street a very poor young man who was in love. His hat was old, his coat worn, his cloak was out at the elbows, the water passed through his shoes—and the stars through his soul."

~ Victor Hugo, *Les Misérables*

The Lucid Zone
(or Middle Way)

In his book *Zen and the Brain* James Austin outlines the levels of consciousness a meditator passes through on the way to nirvana and beyond to the state of Ongoing Enlightenment Traits (see the diagram on the next page). The first four levels represent increasing states of concentration. At levels V and VI, an array of pleasurable moods is experienced, from equanimity and contentment to joy, euphoria and ecstasy. The levels below the dotted line can be enjoyed during normal waking reality; the levels above are intense rarified states of consciousness that remove one from any semblance of normal waking reality. One can't drive a car here.

Where we want to be in our everyday lives is in the zone of Pleasurable Moods.

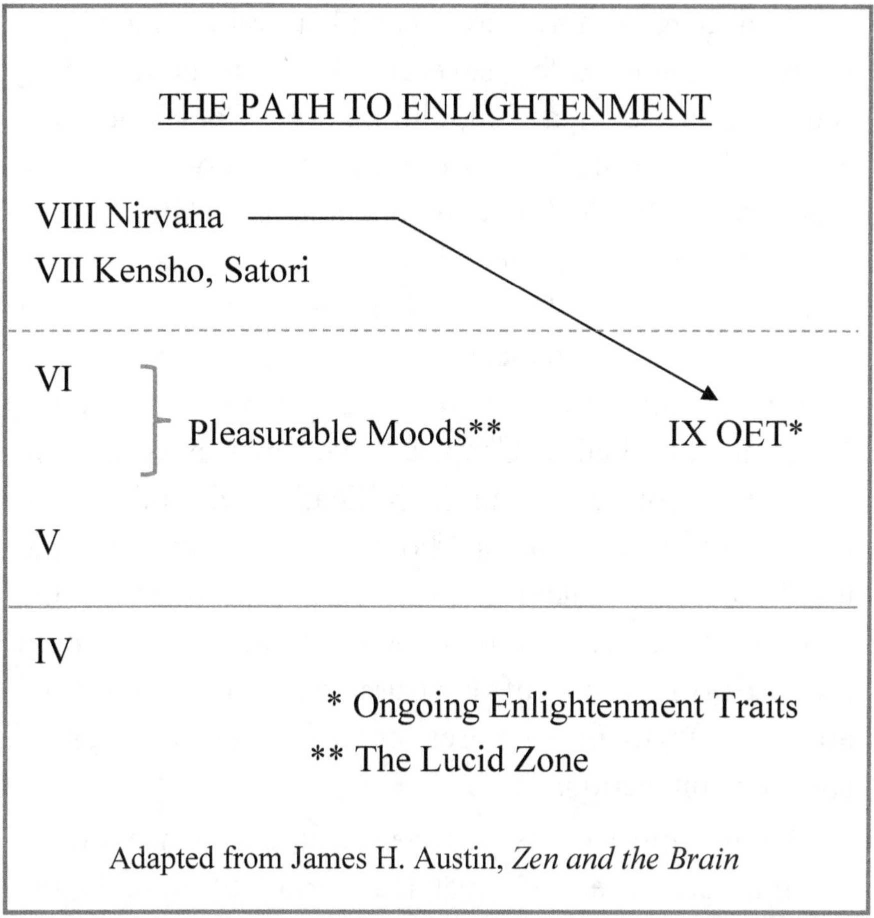

What I propose is that a regular practice of Lucid Focusing will raise your General Mood into the pleasurable moods of levels V and VI and that these may become at least regular or even semi-permanent (at least on the lower levels). For future reference I am calling these levels the Lucid Zone.

And there is more here. The pleasurable moods will likely be attended by several other affects including "connection," compassion, and humor. Connection and compassion are different from the other moods because they have both a feeling component and a relational one. With increasing compassion, you will have more concern for the welfare of others because you will feel closer to them. Connection with other people is also known as empathy. If you spent some time in the Moment described in Chapter 1, you may have already recognized your elemental identification with others and their own senses of selfhood. It is known that mindfulness (Lucid Focusing) produces the neurotransmitters, serotonin and oxytocin. Serotonin produces the scale of pleasurable moods mentioned above. Oxytocin increases empathy and feelings of spiritual connection.

I think most of us experience some connection, or communion, when we spend a period of time in the woods. One's consciousness seems to expand into the surroundings. I experienced a profound soul-shaking sense of connection in India. A yoga teacher gave me a mantra (*sri ram jai ram jai jai ram*) to meditate on and I spent the next few days repeating it in my head over and over, walking, eating, and sitting still. On the third day, in the afternoon, I walked into a non-descript field and something extraordinary happened. In a flash, everything suddenly looked different. All the filters were gone. All the qualities of the wildlife around me, the shapes, the colors and the contours were suddenly rheostatically enhanced. And a deep feeling of connection arose within me. It seems trite to say it, but I had merged with the world around me. This is what I wrote at the time.

Suddenly, I am there! In a fleeting moment between the frames of consciousness the union of the world and my self is complete. There is now only vision and the fascination flowing into it. In that moment, the sirens of nature, buried beneath the mantle of these rustic grasses ripped open their petticoats for me to see.

I am transfixed. World that I could explain!

There is no one about, not in the plantations leeward nor on the hillocks rolling up behind; just me in this private Eden of weeds. I fall headfirst into their world, a guest or diplomat from beyond the veil.

A cochineal dye stains the boscage here and there interspersed with clans of green and amber, stratum and substratum, bent over in humility beneath the taller shoots topped with noduled microphones. I wade into the higher growths, a wagging sea of thorns, beads, and leafy fronds, to see hoppers and flies and strange bugs marked with tribal faces on their still wings. Two fliers conjugate, tail to tail, pulling each other from shade to shadow while a grasshopper watches with wide face(na)ted eyes.

Here in the cotton rows I peel back the layers of *maya* to reveal the cosmic fleece. As each pocket bursts open, the silky mesh crystallizes instantly in a soft spray of photons. Airborne, the ivory filaments glance needle-like coruscations from their wafting arcs. Soon I am lost to the miracle of this brief blizzard and the anomalies of cosmic expression. In every subtle yawn and itch of nature is a magnificence shielded by insouciance.

Beyond the cotton fields the millet stalks, a closely knit colony of leaves hissing against each other and cobs nodding listlessly in the heat. I press a cob against my nose and inhale its earthy fume, reminiscent of the must stirred by some previous sub-conscious impulse. The snuff fills my lungs and begins spinning me around on the track between the stalks, folding the sea of millet onto the inner surface of my cylinder of sight.

I am drunk with life! I spin the universe around on its axis, feeling a surge of friction on my extremities. My outstretched hands pulse with the force and my head becomes charged with being. The fields blend into a wash of leafy green weaving time into a static web.

I come to a stop laughing with exhaustion. In the innards of my being there lives a new presence, an invigorating exaltation of the power in latent energy. I look up and find a new miracle.

At the edge of the millet, heralding an open field, a tree throws itself out of the ground with fireworks. The branches lunge into the sky in a viridescent blast that twinkles with lemon stars. I drop on my knees before this vision of the Lord and wrap myself in numinous joy.

The merge is complete. I surrender to the pastoral vision giving up doubt and impatience, laying down at the feet of the Lord the boscage of selves now numbed with their own frivolity.

And away against the cerulean loft of the temple, clouds of uncertain course hold promise of vistas yet to come...

Imagine the neurotransmitters! Mindfulness can produce levels of concentrated awareness approaching what Austin calls *kensho*, which he describes as the "awareness of Suchness, One-ness ... perfection in all things just as they are."[10] Apparently, *kensho* can occur spontaneously anywhere. Austin describes his own experience of *kensho* on the ground level platform of a London subway station. Characterized by the usual dissolution of cognition and the sense of self, Austin's consciousness seemed to fuse with the outer world. With meaning, purpose, value, significance, association (and so on) in suspension, everything reverted back to the simplicity of just being. Everything became, in Kant's terminology, the things-in-themselves ("suchness"). "The glimpse into eternity," Austin wrote, "comes as the most incredible surprise, and it exerts an immensely powerful influence on one's long-range attitudes. It is a realm of the 'always so,' not only the 'just so.' *It is a world of ever thusness. It presumes no moment of creation, no creator, no specific force.*"[11]

The world unfiltered: now it all just is. It is a state of perfect contiguity, without any thoughts about it. We were all born from a state of fusion with our mothers; who knows what elemental imprints remain latent within the psyche? Are they the source of our feelings of connection and on up, our feelings of empathy, compassion and the merging with the world? Empathy is stepping inside another's shoes and understanding what they are feeling. Compassion requires something more: doing something for the benefit of the other— selflessly. At the level of the OET, Austin says, compassion is *"automatic."*[12] It has become an integral part of who one is. At this level, "all beings are one and the same... Now, *self = other* ... the once-isolated human being has finally entered into the ultimate human equation."[13]

Although Austin wrote that achieving this stage requires "decades" of meditative practice, Lucid Focusing and other forms of mindfulness will produce (at least temporary) feelings of connection and compassion within a relatively short time. Abundant research demonstrates that various forms of meditation produce changes in areas of the brain that coordinate with, among other things, the experience of compassion.[14] For instance, brain matter in the area of the temporoparietal junction—which "plays a central role in empathy and compassion"— is increased during meditation.[15]

Lucid Zone Affects

Moods	Relationship	Energy
Ecstasy	Spirituality	Humor
Joy	Compassion	Play
Elation	Empathy	Spontaneity
Contentment	Connection	
Equanimity		

Further, the euphoric connection (with perhaps feelings of compassion) experienced at the higher reaches of the Lucid Zone, may easily be described as "spiritual." Spiritual feelings are real. It's when the reifying motor of the mind grinds out some sort of explanation that things become difficult. Even reifying "spirit" into some sort of substance that extends beyond the body is going too far. Spiritual feelings should be enjoyed for what they are without trying to explain them.

The mind is the playground, capable of a wondrous array of experiences that make this life, its Predicament and its pain, bearable. Beyond the heady feelings at the top end of the pleasure scale and the joy in more intimate connections with others and the natural world, there's the mystery, the intrigue, and the question of what vistas are still to come. At any rate, *kensho* and beyond are available to us all, but where we want to be in our daily lives is in the conscious states just below—sub-*kensho*—or the Lucid Zone, for a few important reasons.

1. They are relatively easy to achieve.
2. They are perfectly compatible with our daily lives.
3. They can be sustained for extended periods of time (if not semi-permanently).

However, while the upper reaches of euphoria can seem like an enlightened state, more is needed. As Austin defined it, the OET is characterised by an extinguishment of various impediments, including cravings and aversions. This is where the exercises outlined in Chapters 10 and 11 come into play. The exercises were designed to extinguish the impediments we acquire in our lives such as shame, guilt, triggers, fear of rejection, negative self-evaluations, cravings, and many others. Each of these has a structure at least partially imprinted by our upbringing and other experiences with the world. In general, the method is to become conscious of the structures and then "deconstruct" them.

For instance, fear of rejection, the shadow side of approval seeking, has a somewhat complex structure. On the one hand, rejection "triggers" what I call the "shame file" (which will be explored in Chapter 7). Deconstructing the shame file (Chapter 11) is one method for becoming free of the fear of rejection. Another is to see how being rejected is a trigger for those devastating feelings that probably stem from long ago when being exiled from the tribe meant certain death. (Being rejected feels like death, doesn't it?) In any case, in the exercise presented in Chapter 11 one fully imagines being rejected and then brings Lucid Focusing to bear on the triggered feeling—until it dissolves. One might need to repeat this exercise a few times, but eventually the associated feeling dissolves for good. And then you are free of it and possibly also free of approval seeking. What should follow is that your controls on acting a certain way in the company of others dissipate and you are much freer to be your spontaneous self. As with most of the material presented in these pages, you know you have "arrived" when you see the humor in it all. "I used to fear being rejected; that's simply a hilarious marvel now!" It's the sound of freedom.

In Austin's words, "A person might be most ready to laugh when every pretense about reality finally vanishes."[16]

Lucid Focusing works to tune one's General Mood toward the Lucid Zone; the exercises remove the baggage that gets in the way. Together, they put one on the path to enlightened spontaneity and playfulness.

You can try Lucid Focusing right now.

Relax the body, focus on what you feel, accept the feeling, and stop thinking (as much as possible). What you should discover is that the feeling you are focused on dissolves and results in an improvement in your General Mood. Lucid Focusing is presented in detail in Chapter 10.

I became convinced that Lucid Focusing was a powerful tool when I applied it to my negative moods and feelings and discovered that the action dissolved them and ushered in level V moods. Continued practice eventually resulted in the negative feelings clearing almost immediately and a subsequent boost in my General Mood on up to the higher stages where it lingered for longer periods of time. As you will see, the application to negative moods and feelings is just the beginning.

The Middle Way refers to Buddha's teaching to live between the extremes, between (for instance) asceticism and pleasure-seeking. Since then the term has been applied to any conflict seeking a moderate resolution. Here, the term simply means the meditative path between normal waking reality (NWR) with its automatic stream of consciousness and the higher states of meditation which are difficult to achieve and unsustainable in NWR. Pema Chödrön, an American Buddhist nun, has a definition that closely describes the drift in these pages.

> "The Middle Way is wide open, but it's tough going, because it goes against the grain of an ancient neurotic pattern that we all share. When we feel lonely, when we feel hopeless, what we want to do is move to the right or the left. We don't want to sit and feel what we feel. We don't want to go through the detox. Yet the Middle Way encourages us to do just that. It encourages us to awaken the bravery that exists in everyone without exception, including you and me."[17]

At this point, I think we should spend some time appreciating the empire of pain we live in.

Chapter 5

"For we are born in others' pain
And perish in our own."
~ Francis Thompson, "Daisy"

Pain

This book is about freedom from emotional pain. Physical pain is a completely different topic. Nevertheless, after doing the exercises presented here, you may find your experiences of physical pain easier to handle.

Emotional pain comes in many varieties: fear, anger, shame, guilt, rejection, loss, jealousy, envy, sadness, despair, hopelessness, depression, loneliness, boredom, and—my favorite—the abject feeling of being lost in a Void.

Pain spreads across the universe. We are minds at the effect of our surroundings. We struggle to cope; we try to understand just what we are involved with here. And we come up empty. The whole shebang seems designed to make us suffer.

First, there is the existential predicament we find ourselves in. The human condition is centered on a consciousness that is unable to fully grasp the situation it is in: embarked on a volcanic orb floating in space with no apparent origin or destination, no apparent meaning or purpose, and no answers to why and how. Steven Weinberg, the Nobel Laureate in physics, once described the earth as "a tiny part of an overwhelmingly hostile universe." "The more the universe seems comprehensible," he lamented, "the more it also seems pointless."[18] Essentially, the human condition is to be eternally uncertain and terrified. It brings to mind the idiosyncratic words of T. S. Eliot:

> Go, go, go, said the bird: human kind
> Cannot bear very much reality.[19]

The fear of death is the foundation for all our other fears; we can't help but recognize our vulnerability. Freud thought that it was woven into our cells. We don't dwell on it, but our eventual death remains the one certainty in our lives. It lingers at the base of our consciousness and rises up like a phantasm whenever we are in danger. It's probably the most wrenching feeling in our repertoire of emotional pain.

In an article in *American Psychologist*, the evolutionary psychologist, David Buss, theorized that emotional pain is built into the system as a survival strategy. The fear of death, for instance, is accompanied by an injection of adrenalin into the system in order to fight or flee with a burst of energy. And many others, including psychological pain, anxiety, depression, certain fears, phobias, and jealousy, arise from various "psychological mechanisms that are 'designed' to cause subjective stress under some circumstances."[20] Jealousy, for instance, evolved as a means of combatting the threat to mating for the long term. "If these hypotheses are correct," Buss writes, "they suggest that part of the operation of the normal psychological machinery *inevitably* entails experiencing psychological distress in certain contexts."[21]

Second, the cultural surround works its nearly imperceptible alchemy on us. Western culture (at least) is experiencing a slowly evolving disconnection with community and traditional values. We are becoming more and more alienated, from nature and each other. Our critical sense of belonging is weakening. The pain of loneliness afflicts the entire culture. It has been happening at least as far back as the Age of Enlightenment when the "individual" began to take pre-eminence over the tribe. And it has happened so slowly that we couldn't possibly notice how it has affected us. But we sense something is missing. What it is is intimacy, physical touch, a strong kinship, a certain sense of belonging, social bonds, and "unconditional positive regard." But we don't really know it. It's all too far gone. Now factor into our ambiguous malaise an enveloping culture that values human beings based on their wealth, power, and fame (okay, also talent). What that means for the rest of us is a core feeling of inadequacy. Our self-evaluations always come up short against the celebrated.

Continuing with the catalogue of emotional pain, we are obliged to factor in other human beings. Collectively, people only increase both our sense of uncertainty and our fear. Being with others and dealing with their own uncertainties and fears means being at the effect of mendacity, manipulation, venality, jealousy, rejection, disapproval, envy, and so on. We trigger each other and it goes on all day long. At its worst, we are victims of institutionalised oppression, racism, genderism, and economic inequality. In spite of being in the same boat, cosmically speaking, human beings are inclined to exert their power over each other. The shared consciousness of the planet has to be affected on some level by the wars, the atrocities, the wholesale killing, the refugees, the rampant corruption, and sheer viciousness of much of the human race. It's all extremely depressing.

And then there's unrequited love, unrequited desire, and perhaps the most painful feeling of them all: utter devastation when the person you love more than anything in this world leaves you for another.

The scheme presented in these pages wouldn't be credible if it was incapable of diminishing most of these emotional pains. The following is an account of an experience I had that convinced me that Lucid Focusing works at the deepest level of pain.

About a month after I had filed for bankruptcy, a woman who I loved from the core of my soul and considered an important, if not essential part of my life, texted me that she had met the love of her life. In a few moments, I collapsed inside. The thought that I would never see her again devastated me. My emotional temper sank lower and lower until I realized that I had never experienced, never even conceived of, such an abject level of pain. Not even my experience of the Void, which I will explore more fully below, came even close to this depth of despair. And I thought that I would never be able to shake it. The situation was simply unresolvable. As long as the situation persisted—certainly forever, so I thought—I would be in the grip of this demonic Knot. And soon I began to think that if it persisted for a few days, the thought of suicide would surely be in the mix. Really. I could not contemplate going through life gripped by this unbearable pain. I left home to buy some alcohol and cigars. What did anything matter anymore?

But then the thought came that all I had left was the Meta-View and Lucid Focusing. I really did not think that the process could possibly dissolve this deepest level of devastation. But it was all I had (besides the alcohol and cigars). So I shifted into a determined focus on the feeling. I walked around the park in the neighbourhood looking at the feeling, trying my best to stop thinking about it, forcing the Meta-View, falling back, shifting back again. It took about two hours, but the feeling did slowly dissipate into one of well, I would call it, resolution, or buoyancy, or a sense that I could cope with it. It wasn't a full liberation from the feeling, but it was like I had at least risen to the surface again. I was no longer drowning. In the next few days acceptance of the situation became more grounded and I was able to function almost normally again. The take away was that the process had been tested at the darkest corners of the mind and really did work. And this thought produced a sweet elation.

Ever since this experience I have had near total control over my emotions. After a time of focusing on my feelings and seeing them dissolve, I was able to sweep away fears and anxieties as soon as they arose.

It all begins with feeling bad…..

#   #   #

In the previous chapters, I laid the groundwork for an exploration of the human self. Achieving the enlightened state of mind is not only a process of doing various exercises; it is also one of neutralizing or dissolving various mental structures that weight heavy on the soul. Some of these are our self-evaluations. Clarifying the enormous effect that culture has on our self-evaluations is perhaps the first step in seeing them for what they are. We are not at fault for thinking less of ourselves. We're just mistaken.

Accordingly, let's turn to the subject of the self.

Chapter 6

"People will do anything, no matter how absurd, in order to avoid facing their own souls. One does not become enlightened by imagining figures of light, but by making the darkness conscious."

~ Carl Jung, *Psychology and Alchemy*

The Self

The catalogue of the inner theatre begins with our sense of self. This item is the one constant in the inner theatre. We may not always be aware of the *sense* of ourselves, because we are absorbed in other mental processes. In normal waking awareness, our sense of self mingles with all the other stuff going on in our heads—feelings, desires, thoughts, visual imagery, and so on—and usually recedes out of sight. If you are afflicted with tinnitus as I am, you know that although it is always there, you stop being aware of it because you are focused on so many other things. Stop thinking and focus your attention inward and suddenly you are aware of your own consciousness. As we will see, this simple exercise is crucial to what follows.

The term, "sense of self," implies two things: an experience—the sensing—and an imputed thing—what is sensed. The way we experience our mental imagery suggests a core "experiencer" that sees, hears, feels, and so on, and is the locus of the word "I." Descartes intuited that the "I" resided in the pineal gland because of its position right in the centre of the brain.

Brain science, however, tells us that the self is not a thing, it is a mental process. The sense of self comes together from several neural processes rising in concert through the layers of the brain until they become conscious. The neurologist Antonio Damasio describes the processes involved in his best-selling book, *The Feeling of What Happens*. "Core consciousness," he writes, "occurs when the brain's representation devices generate an imaged, nonverbal account of how the organism's own state is affected by the organism's processing of an object...."[22]

Let's take a closer look at what he means.

The brain is essentially an information processing machine. The information comes into the brain from our perceptual organs (as well as from the body's own internal state). Let's take vision as an example. An object is seen, enters the brain through the eyes, where it becomes represented internally by an image. The image impacts an unconscious neural network whose job it is to monitor and regulate the state of the organism. At the same time, the brain represents this entire process in other images including a feeling of knowing – an inner sense of being the knower of the known.

"That inner sense," Damasio says, "conveys a powerful nonverbal message regarding the relationship between the organism and the object; that there is an individual subject in the relationship, a transiently constructed entity to which the knowledge of the moment is seemingly attributed."[23] The sense of self is born and reborn with each new pulse of consciousness, perhaps 10 million times a second.

The imputation of a *tangible* self at the core of consciousness is an example of reification. My dictionary defines reify as "to consider or make (an abstract idea or concept) real or concrete." It is the action of ascribing substance to an insubstantial concept, such as ghosts, time, a core self and enlightenment. It is important for our purposes here because it illustrates how cognition—our thinking processes—ascribes meaning, purpose, qualities, values and so on, to everything in both the external and internal worlds.

David Brooks, the *New York Times* columnist, offers an example of reification in a description of his conversion to Christianity. "I was gripped by the conviction that the people I encountered were not skin bags of DNA," he wrote, "but had souls; had essences with no size or shape, but that gave them infinite value and dignity. The conviction that people have souls led to the possibility that there was some spirit who breathed souls into them."[24] Really? Once the soul is reified into an entity, a *thing*, it becomes transferable (by the breath in this case). That's the critical operation because being transferable, it suggests that the soul is capable of surviving death.

In the previous chapter I made the point that the human condition teeters on a series of provocative yet unanswerable questions. This creates a robust market for (ostensible) answers, in particular about human origins, meaning, purpose, and the questions why and how. Narratives emerge to compensate for the existential predicament. Worlds are created. Hope, which springs eternal, turns promises into beliefs. Religion galvanizes lost souls. And it's all based on the reification of a fog of fantasies, one of them being the soul.

The function of cognition is to make sense of the world. It does this first by representing everything it encounters with an image or a word or both. A representational model of the world, called the schema, is formed and every new item encountered is examined to see how it "fits in" with the current model. Not only that, each item is tagged with an attribute along scales of right and wrong, good and bad, and others. These operations all help to make sense of both the external and internal worlds.

Eventually, the intuited core self must be assimilated into the schema (which may be called one's POV). And so it acquires its own attributes, characteristics, and properties. Some of these may be structural (or cosmic) like when we imagine that the core self is a soul with substance. And they may be attended by visual imagery. (I imagine mine as a glowing amber blob.)

This is a critical point in understanding ourselves. There is the *experience* of the self, as it is lived, and there is its *representation* in the schema, as it is thought about. Nothing in the core self's representation is true, unless it is limited to the one statement that "the self has no 3rd Person objective status." That is, unlike a rock or a tree, it can't be viewed, handled, or measured in any way. It is a purely subjective—1st Person—entity. It wallows up from the gnarly folds of the brain and at the nexus of perception and memory it becomes the core of our experience; it becomes who we are at the source. This was the revolutionary discovery of Buddha, who saw the critical difference between the experience and the representation of the self. He saw that who we *think* we are (as opposed to *who we are*) is the source of the existential problem.

As soon as you ascribe some sort of substance to the soul, and then some attributes to it, you have committed to the cognitive error of reification. David Brooks reified the soul in several steps. First, he gave it a name ("soul"), then he ascribed to it some kind of "essence," then he imagined that it could be exhaled from one entity to another, and finally he attributed to it the qualities of "pure goodness, pure loving kindness, holiness." For Brooks, this soul construction answers his "Who am I?" question. But it really only answers his "Who do I *think* I am?" question. None of what he thinks about the soul is true. The "soul" is a biological function that produces a sense of selfhood which looks back on itself and vainly tries to find its source and grasp it. And that's the end of it.

To illustrate this further, imagine that you have taken a psychedelic drug and your soul appears in your mind. Let's say it is a white pulsing sphere. You think, "That's my soul!" But then you suddenly realize that if that's your soul, who or what is looking at it? The historical analogy is the philosopher David Hume's quest for his own soul. When he went looking for it, he came up with nothing beyond "some particular perception or other, of heat or cold, light or shade, love or hatred, pain or pleasure." "I never can catch *myself* at any time," he wrote, "without a perception, and never can observe anything but the perception."[25] Another analogy would be a flashlight attempting to shine its beam on its source. Hume couldn't find his self (as an object) in the inner theatre because it was the very thing looking for it.

Seeing—conceptualizing—the core self as a phenomenological effect devoid of substance created by the brain is the first step on the road to liberation.

The sense of a *fons et origo* of experience is, of course, not the *self at large.* When we talk about ourselves, we are almost always referring to the whole person: body, behavior, character, disposition, sexual orientation, and so on. We may call it the extended self. It is an interactive dynamic of personal tastes, interests, skills, and worldview, and the contents of consciousness such as thoughts, feelings, and desires, as well as our assessments about all of these, including general self-regard. The content of the extended self answers the question: "Who are you?"

Many who study and write about the subject believe that the extended self is wholly a creation of culture. To get a sense of this, imagine that you were born in Medieval times (say in England) or in modern times in rural Namibia. Applying all the items in the catalogue, think about how different you would be.

The psychologist, Philip Cushman, describes the current (Western) extended self as "bounded" (or individualistic), "masterful" (responsible), and "empty."

> [O]ur terrain has shaped a self that experiences a significant absence of community, tradition, and shared meaning.

It experiences these social absences and their consequences 'interiorly' as a lack of personal conviction and worth, and it embodies the absences as a chronic, undifferentiated emotional hunger. The post-World War II self thus yearns to acquire and consume as an unconscious way of compensating for what has been lost: It is empty.[26]

It is empty in part because of the loss of family, community, and tradition. It is a self that seeks the experience of being continually filled up by consuming goods, calories, experiences, politicians, romantic partners, and empathetic therapists in an attempt to combat the growing alienation and fragmentation of its era. This response has been implicitly prescribed by a post-World War II economy that is dependent on the continual consumption of nonessential and quickly obsolete items and experiences.[27]

"Empty" is clearly metaphorical, but even then it is too extreme. The extended self always has some sort of content. Incomplete is perhaps more accurate. Or insufficient. Or flawed. It's the proverbial hole in the soul. It's the feeling of not being good enough. Let's take a closer look at the structure of this flaw. There is a core *feeling* of lacking something. And there is the *judgment* that you're not good enough. Judgments, however, imply some sort of justification, a standard against which something can be reliably measured. In this case, the standard is comparative, not static. That is, compared with the successful, wealthy, and powerful, you haven't got a chance.

This warrants further examination. Everyone knows Marlon Brando's lament in the movie, *On the Waterfront*: "I coulda been somebody." Which translates as, "I'm still a nobody." Another cultural trope is the expression, "*amounting* to something." It implies that until you are successful, you amount to nothing. *You have no substance.* These cultural myths saturate the social fabric. In a binary world, "somebody" has a value of 1; "nobody" has a value of zero. This is reification at its most diabolical. Words construct worlds. They establish values. Success, wealth, fame or a high-status lover raises the value of one's being, both in the eyes of the public and in one's own self-assessment. The problem is this: the modern ego is obsessed with the reification of something that is essentially *unreifiable*. The core self is a brain process; the extended self is a cultural construction. Neither are tangible entities. The core self is the legend in our own minds; the extended self is the *Divine Comedy*. Self-worth is only quantifiable in comparison with others. But no matter what the standard of measurement is, in whichever culture you choose, it is all made up. It's a ghost.

So now we know that our self-assessments are simply not true. Even in those cases where we think of ourselves as high status beings, the elucidation of the structure of this thought brings it all crashing down. It's a hilarious nonsense.

Here's the *Divine Comedy*. Our self-evaluation is the basis of our relationship with ourselves. On its face, this may sound paradoxical. How can I be in relationship with myself? But it is true. The creation of an extended self sets this situation up from first principles. We live with a shade of opinion about ourselves somewhere on the scale of like/dislike, approve/disapprove (and which may easily vary throughout the day). A person, a consciousness, can actually hate itself. When you look at this situation clinically, a human consciousness in violent opposition to itself, is certainly ironic, if not quite humorous. But of course, it is fairly widespread among the human population. Here it is important to add that even the situation of a consciousness liking itself has its comical side, especially when it has risen to the level of acute narcissism. (Being at peace with oneself is something else.) The only way to make sense of a negative self-appraisal is to see it as resulting from some sort of illusion, an illusion generated from the very creation of and structure of the extended self.

This illusion is the assumption of some semblance of truth in our self-assessments. That is, the statements, "I am bad"; "I am a failure"; "I am not worth much"; and so on, have validity (our sense of self-worth is assumed to be *true*), when in fact they have no validity whatsoever. (It is also true that the positive self-appraisals are equally illusory—or perhaps more accurately, contrived—but they are much healthier ones to have.) Our self-assessments are all arbitrary; that is, they are not woven into the fabric of the universe. They are all *constructions*—or reifications. They are all, to borrow a concept, *maya*.

The extent to which we buy into the illusion is the extent to which we diminish our self-evaluations. We can't help but compare ourselves to the rich, famous and powerful, based on culturally-defined standards. Seeing culturally-defined standards as arbitrary (not to mention, fraught with error) is a first step in ceasing to buy into them—at least where one's self-evaluation is concerned. And then to recognize that much of our emotional pain results from the mistaken assumption of the truth of these culturally-defined standards of measurement.

In his seminal exploration of the self, Anthony Brandt came to this rather sobering conclusion:

> A man struggles to rise in order to win the Other's envy and esteem, to persuade society, and thereby himself, that he is somebody. In the process he becomes an object to himself, acts from a center outside himself: from the imagined, feared heart of the Other.[28]

When you get to the other side, and you see the structure underpinning what you think about yourself, you won't be able to avoid seeing the humor. That's the *Divine Comedy* (or the Cosmic Joke).

It's no secret that compared with the rich, famous and powerful the rest of us feel "lesser" in some unquantifiable way. Besides the greater talent (often true perhaps) there is an aura around them that both raises them above and distances them from the rest of us. Even with all the exposés about celebrities having a terrible time with themselves, the fantasy of what that life could be for *us* is an overpowering thought. And we all share in it (most of us anyway). The good news is that although we may never achieve celebrityhood, we can eliminate the envy of it. It should be fairly easy to do since the envy is just a culturally-created conscious response.   And when you see the structure of the conscious response, essentially an edifice of values, you may see that it is all a house of cards.

A major component of the structure is our "absorption" in it. We live it without noticing the cause and effect, the values, and so on. When we see the structure, including our absorption in it, we have "risen above it." This is called the Meta-View and it will be explored at length below. Its importance is that from the Meta-View one can begin to dissolve the structures that prevent our finding the free and spontaneous self.

Some paragraphs previously I pointed out that the hole in the soul has a judgment component and a feeling component. Where does the feeling come from? Where does this core sense of incompleteness come from? Much has been written on this question. The reason has been attributed to the structure of the ego, the fear of death, the empty self, and others. But let's consider one other possibility.

Chapter 7

"Anton Checkov once observed that the worst thing life can do to human beings is to inflict humiliation. Nothing, nothing, nothing in the world can destroy the soul as much as outright humiliation. Every other infliction can eventually be withstood or overcome, but not humiliation. Humiliation lingers in the mind, the heart, the veins, the arteries forever. It allows people to brood for decades on end, often deforming their inner lives."[29]

Shame

Shame is a rather odd emotion. It is clearly one of those "relationship with the self" feelings, like guilt. And it is not a pleasant one. Among all the emotions in our repertoire, shame is one of the most devastating. Plunged into an experience of shame, you are naked and all eyes are burning right through your sense of self. Even if you do not agree with the judgements levied against you, you will likely still feel their weight. But in the case where you are aligned with others' condemnation of you—when you agree with them—it's a deep, dark abyss from which there appears to be no escape.

We endure shame without ever asking what it is all about. We just assume that it is natural, and therefore appropriate. And furthermore, that its assumptions are true.

Here, we should distinguish between shame and guilt. Guilt is usually about what we have done; shame is about who we are. But we can clearly be ashamed about what we have done and feel guilty about what we are ashamed of. Both these emotions are considered to be socially constructed. That is, we are not born with them, like fear, anger, joy and so on. So where does shame come from?

I had an intuition that shameful experiences might chain back one from the other to a very early time in my life and I became interested to see if I could access in memory my first shameful experience. Further if I could "neutralize" that experience so it no longer held any effect on me, the others might tumble like a house of cards. That was my working hypothesis. This is what I wrote about it in an unpublished memoir:

> I sat down at the kitchen table, closed my eyes, calmed my mind, and probed for a recent shame event. Thinking about this years later, I can't remember what first came up but the chain regressed through the dark ages of teenage acne ("a conspiracy in every pore" is how I put it looking in the mirror), my father scorning my tight pants as being

too "revealing," my mother confronting me with tracings of naked women hidden under my mattress, down through the photograph taken at a friend's birthday party, where I grimaced just as the camera snapped (a scandal up and down the block). Eventually I did get to a very primitive level. There was no memory of a specific event, only an archaic feeling of someone pinching my lifeline and a distinct visual image—my mother's look of disapproval. And it came to me, an overwhelming insight into what shame is—ontologically: the feeling that occurs when a mother's love is withdrawn.

I was stunned. I began looking for any corroboration of this idea in the psychological literature. And lo and behold! I found an article by the psychoanalyst, Allan Schore, which described the neonatal rudiments of shame in a child's relationship with its parents.

The neo-individuating self, in a hyperstimulated, elated, grandiose, narcissistically charged state of heightened arousal, exhibits itself during a reunion with the caregiver. Despite an excited anticipation of a shared affect state, the self unexpectedly experiences an affective misattunement, thereby triggering a sudden stress, shock-induced deflation. It is now proposed that this first occurs in the preverbal practicing subphase of the separation-individuation period, and that this specific object relation and its internalization is the prototype of the shame experience.[30]

Wow. It is thought that every subsequent experience of shame on into adulthood resonates with the feelings associated with this prototypical scenario. But it makes sense. Consider what you feel when you feel shame. You feel abandoned, cut off from the people around you, and from society as a whole. Suddenly all eyes are on you and they are disapproving. You shrink from a state of self-empowerment to one of extreme vulnerability. You are naked and there is no escape. Just like that young toddler who has suddenly (momentarily) lost the loving lifeline (the attunement) with its mother.

It can't all be pinned on mother. Most psychologists are of the view that shame originates in the early family at about the age of two. So it is likely that both parents are guilty. Many psychologists believe that shame's relative severity correlates with the severity of one's upbringing (from both parents). An upbringing characterized by regimentation, control, an emphasis on achievement, and/or a lack of feeling or touch will produce more shame than one on the opposite end of the scale. Psychologists have known for several decades that "physical contact and touch are the most powerful and profound affect regulators creating a sense of safeness and comfort."[31]

> Even when parents are not overtly abusive or neglectful, and indeed may be highly motivated to be good parents, shame can introduce distortions in the child-parent relationship that have long-term impacts. Furthermore, because these effects are subtle, children growing up with parents who carry a lot of shame may be unaware of the degree to which their development is being influenced by parental shame and may themselves be highly vulnerable to shame later in life.[32]

> Western culture is putting growing emphasis on socially comparative, competitive driven parenting. The advent of 'how to do books' increases parental concern to do the 'right thing' for their child, and increases various fears of being incompetent in the role, and entice parents to constantly monitor themselves to the standards they are supposed to be meeting, especially but not only in

comparison with others. ... [Their child's] misbehavior in public or not achieving academically is seen to reflect shame on them. Some parents are in competition with their parenting peers, invest[ing] heavily in the child to maximize success and achievement above all else. Indeed, correlational studies have found a strong focus on goals like status and money (compared with community feeling) are associated with being less warm and more controlling towards one's children.[33]

One psychologist wrote that "parenting," a concept developed during the 1960s "indicates a desire or goal to turn the child into 'something,' and there is some kind of outcome to be achieved, which is one-directional."[34] This is nothing short of the reification of the child. I can hear Melanie singing, "Look what they've done to my song, Ma." The stunning fact is that the vast majority of parents experience some degree of shame much of the time. According to a recent (U.S.) study, "90% of mothers and 85% of fathers felt judged by strangers and other parents, with 50% reporting feeling judged almost all of the time, and first-time mothers experience shame and judgment from the earliest moments of motherhood in connection with childbirth and infant feeding."[35]

As has already been noted, the withering of traditional communities has produced a culture of increasing individualism and alienation, and a shift in values (and self-evaluations) towards success, wealth and fame, making fertile ground for the inculcation of shame across the population.

You can hear the gravity in the words of psychologist Robert Karen when he wrote: "Who can emerge from childhood without some susceptibility to feelings of defect, especially in certain threatening contexts? We all have shadow portraits of the self we'd rather not look at and habits of being we cling to in order to keep shame at bay."[36]

Those shadow portraits, I call the shame file. Our parents, to some degree, controlled our behavior by threatening to trigger our shame files (often subtly). The trigger is the withdrawal of their love or "unconditional positive regard." It's just that simple, the more so at younger ages. When we are older we discover on the schoolyard that the surrounding culture threatens to trigger us at any moment. Shame becomes the albatross around our necks, seemingly a permanent fixture. Perhaps a metaphor of equal force is the sword of Damocles, hovering by a thread, always primed to pierce our hearts.

Clearly shame qualifies as the source of the hole in the soul.

But it's not a hole. The self is not empty; it is at war with itself. It doesn't really like itself.

The award-winning writer, Joan Didion, said it this way: "Once, in a dry season, I wrote in large letters across two pages of a notebook that innocence ends when one is stripped of the delusion that one likes oneself."[37]

The question becomes, is there a way out? The cultural barb of achieving success, wealth, power or fame is geared toward filling the hole, rather than brokering an armistice, and perhaps for that reason, it does not work. Testimonials from many super-achievers tell us this is so. Sammy Davis, Jr., for instance, once reflected on his success. "First making it big," he said, "it's like being twenty-one. You're on top of the hill. This is what I've fought for all my life. I've got the success and I've licked the critics in New York. Now why the fuck ain't I happy?"[38]

Sue Erikson Bloland is the daughter of Erik Erikson, the famed developmental psychologist. An integrative psychotherapist and psychoanalyst herself, Bloland wrote an in-depth article in *The Atlantic* about her father's extensive insecurities in spite of being at the zenith of his profession.

Fame is not a successful defense against
feelings of inadequacy. It only appears to

be. This is where the greatest distortion lies in our idealization of the famous. We imagine that our heroes have transcended the adversities of the human condition and have healed their childhood traumas by achievement of the extraordinary. We want to believe that they have arrived at a secure place of self-approval; that achieving recognition—success—can set us free from gnawing feelings of self-doubt. We want to believe that if we ourselves could just secure enough recognition and approval from the outside world, if we could feel sufficiently admired, we would be healed and our self-esteem secured. Like the celebrities we admire so much, we would be rescued from the relentless need for validation.[39]

The hole in the soul is not easily filled. The self simply cannot acquire the elusive substance it seeks. If one never reaches the point of "enough," then one will continue on a path of "more"—indefinitely. It might be called compulsive venality. In spite of winning a Pulitzer (for the book, *Ghandi's Truth*), Erikson yearned for the Nobel until the day he died.

An alternative method to filling the hole is simply to dissolve it.

The story here thus far is to demonstrate that our self-evaluations (including our shame) are constructions, reifications, etchings. They have been highly influenced by what surrounds us. They are, in a word, arbitrary. They are groundless. And thus they are susceptible to change.

Becoming conscious of the structure is the first step in changing it. Seeing your self-evaluations change from true to highly suspect, or even to completely bogus, means that they can be replaced with new ones—or, most intriguing of all, done away with completely.

You arrive at a place where your self-evaluations are minimal, if at all. You just are—without attributes.

Imagine that you have eliminated all shame from your extended self. You have no issues with yourself anymore. You are free of approval-seeking, fear of disapproval, rejection, insult, and fault-finding. No one can trigger your shame button any more. Any attempts to trigger you, such as insulting you, are seen as an opportunity to play. One response could be: "Well, how did you become so perceptive, especially when you haven't got a clue who you are?"

Eventually, whenever a negative self-appraisal comes up, you will respond with the thought, "I don't have to think like this anymore. This is merely programming that I can change." Furthermore, when you *believe* that you don't have to think like that, the negative thought will almost immediately dissolve. And when you see the humor in having actually placed credence in your self-evaluations, in having reified appraisals of the self and the self itself, you are free.

The exploration of the self—how our representations of the world are sometimes reified (or constructed), and our resulting self-evaluations are based on standards which are culturally influenced—underscores the fact that our self-evaluations can simply be changed into ones that are more positive—or even non-existent. At the stage where they have become non-existent, we become simply what we are, without attribution, without even definition. We become liberated from all judgement, approval and disapproval, both within and the world outside.

THE CATALOGUE

of the Inner Theatre

Chapter 8

Inside Our Heads – The Contents of Consciousness

Primary Content

The following is only a partial list of what goes on inside our heads, but these are the main events:

1. Thoughts
2. Feelings
3. Cravings (Desires)
4. Sensations
5. Visual Imagery
6. The Sense of Self
7. The Schema (our worldview, beliefs, construals)

Our emotional pain is mostly a product of the first three, so I will concentrate on them.

1. Thoughts: the stream of thinking, reasoning, logic, figuring things out.

2. Feelings are of two main types:

   A. Triggered or reactive Feelings
   B. General Mood

A. Triggered feelings arise in response to both external and internal stimuli. They include anger, hate, fear, shame, guilt, joy, elation, surprise, and so on. They are essentially primitive responses programmed into our nervous systems to make us pay attention to significant events in our surroundings.

Much of our lives is about disappointment, regret, and fear, mostly negative and painful stuff. There are twice as many types of negative feelings as there are positive ones. This may have had survival benefits in the past, but today, most of what makes us feel bad needn't be so.

There are three important aspects of our feelings. One is that they are largely (if not completely) influenced by culture. Two is that even within cultures, most feeling responses are essentially arbitrary. For instance, just because you are alone, you don't necessarily have to feel lonely. You may have nothing to do, but you don't have to feel bored. When someone rejects you, you don't have to feel rejection, anger or shame. You may think that experiencing fear when confronted by a predatory animal is hard-wired, but there are many examples of animal experts who swim with crocodiles, wrestle with wild lions, and know how to handle a threatening polar bear. Our feeling reactions are essentially arbitrary, contingent, variable, and both socially and culturally influenced or constructed.

When you see and understand this fact more fully, each time you experience a negative feeling you will be primed to go into the Meta-View. And the more you shift into the Meta-View whenever a negative feeling comes up, your programmed reactions to particular situations will lessen and eventually completely dissolve. These days, I am not much affected by another's disapproval, rejection, anger, disappointment, and so on. And these are major changes in my life.

Imagine the situation where you are being fired from a job you've had for fifteen years. Your emotional reactions (fear, anger, shame) may well be appropriate to the situation, but they are not hard-wired. You could conceivably respond with a loud belly-laugh. You could jump for joy. You could look at your boss with compassion because you understand his position. I know there are dire circumstances relating to one's survival in the real world. Laughing in the face of adversity may not be possible right now. But it can be done. My intention here is to demonstrate that *it is possible to have a different emotional response in almost any situation.*

The third aspect is that Lucid Focusing demonstrates that feelings can be dissolved at will.

B. Our General Mood is how we feel when we are not experiencing a triggered Feeling. It is our default in conscious awareness. Our General Mood ranges between a very depressed state of mind to the heights of joy. At the top end—the Lucid Zone (Chapter 4)—our moods range between equanimity and contentment to joy and euphoria. This is where we want to be and it is achievable once we understand the mechanisms at work in our consciousness and change how they operate on our default mood.

3. Cravings may be classified into three distinct kinds:

1. Natural desires (for food, water and sex)
2. Desires for acquisition (power, wealth, possessions, fame, and so on)
3. Unwanted Cravings (responses to triggered negative Feelings, a depressed General Mood, or from being addicted to something)

The first two are, relative to the third, not the problem, but let's acknowledge that the natural desire for sex (libido or lust) can be painful when it is unfulfilled.

It is the third one that is problematic. I tried to think of the right term for these cravings—unhealthy, risky, dangerous? However it is conceivable that someone would recognize all of these and want to continue to satisfy the urge anyway. The problematic cravings have to go at some time. The ones to begin with are the ones that you would prefer not to have anymore. They are troubling. Smoking is a perfect example. The craving is overwhelming, the pleasure palpable, and the inner pleas to quit are resounding echoes in the mind. Others are alcohol, junk food, and any obsessions. Unwanted cravings and how to be free of them will be explored in greater detail in Chapter 12.

Secondary Content

The experience of a thought, feeling, craving, (and so on) is attended by some or all of the following secondary aspects of consciousness:

1. Focus
2. Intentionality
3. Resistance
4. Knots
5. Absorption
6. The Meta-View

1. Focus

As long as we are conscious, we are focused on something, usually a combination of the external world and the inner theatre. Our focus sharpens on a select few of the items here according to how we evaluate their importance in the moment and the rest fade toward the background and the peripheries of consciousness. For instance, suddenly faced with a lion in the wild, consciousness zooms in on the lion, fear grips us, and thinking becomes preoccupied with potential escape routes. All other concerns become irrelevant. Closer to home, a triggered feeling such as anger may fill out almost all of our focus. Or we may become lost in thought or overtaken by a craving for something. The significance of focus will be better appreciated when we explore absorption and the Meta-View.

2. Intentionality

This is the philosophical term for the "aboutness" of a mental state. When thinking, we are always thinking *about* something. When absorbed by a triggered feeling, it is usually about the trigger. Similarly, cravings are about what is desired.

What is important here is to see how Lucid Focusing shifts the intentionality from a trigger or a situation to the triggered feeling and sets up a sequence of events leading to the Lucid Zone.

3. Resistance

In my exploration of my feelings, I noticed something rather subtle. Negative feelings in particular were attended by a frisson of resistance, an energy that pushed back against the feeling's full expression. I intuited several possible reasons for this: culturally-instilled self-control; an internal damping effect to safeguard overwhelming the circuitry; the superego's authority over the id; and possibly a general resistance to any change in the usual stream of things.

I entertain a theory that the emotions are messages sent from the lower brain to the higher brain. Their mission is to elicit the felt sense that they have been received, acknowledged and understood. Resistance inhibits this project, extending the duration of the painful feeling and increasing the overall torment of the Knot.

The phenomenon of resistance illustrates the importance of willfully accepting the feeling during Lucid Focusing. Accepting the feeling should immediately produce a diminishment of its intensity as the energy of resistance dissipates.

4. Knots

A Knot is a complex of a (usually) negative feeling and intense thinking. It's a knot because the thinking stimulates the feeling and the feeling fuels the thinking.

For instance, I got off the phone with an online company, after an hour's argument about money they failed to transfer to my account. I got the problem resolved, but the people I talked to—four levels of representatives and supervisors—didn't seem to really understand what should have been a very clear mistake on their part. After I put the phone down, the conversation kept playing over and over again in my mind. My frustration fuelled my thinking about it and my thinking just kept stimulating the frustration. That's the essence of a Knot: emotion and cognition stirring each other up in a seemingly endless vicious cycle. Tweedledum and Tweedledee.

A Knot may be composed of a positive feeling and thoughts, like the memory of the previous night's sexual encounter, but these are not the problem unless they become obsessive. If you cannot stop thinking about something, Lucid Focusing will come to the rescue.

Conceptualizing the Knot complex and catching it in the Meta-View as it happens gives us an opportunity to regain our emotional control. And once we recognize it, we can eliminate various recurrent fears. A useful analogy is found in video editing. A video has at least two tracks, one of which is the audio. The audio track can be unlocked from the video track for editing on its own or to simply dispose of it. In the same way we can unlock the feeling track from the thinking track in the Knot and dispose of the whole thing. The "lock" in a Knot is the culturally-induced buy-in of the appropriateness of the feeling response to a particular situation. I have already mentioned that being alone doesn't mean that we have to feel lonely even though we might easily think that we *should* feel that way.

What about death? It's widely accepted that the appropriate response is fear. The fear of death is a Knot that seems to be locked into our psyches as much as the joy of sex. But is it? If we now know that Lucid Focusing can dissolve the feeling track in a Knot (and consequently the entire complex), all we have to do is apply the exercise to our fear of death and neutralize it— for good. The exercise is presented in Chapter 11. Try it.

Knots generally fall into three main categories: regret about the past, fear of the future, and disappointment about not having something in the present.

5 & 6. Absorption and the **Meta-View** are explored in the next chapter.

Chapter 9

Absorption, the Meta-View and Lucid Focusing

The concept of absorption would be meaningless without its opposite, the unabsorbed state. If we were always absorbed by one or several of the elements in our conscious minds, there would be no mindfulness, introspection, complex insight, or internal intervention. Essentially we would be automatons, moving from one absorbed state to the next. And in fact, that is what we are—*most of the time*. Psychologists call this state of absorption "automaticity" and estimate that human beings spend about 95 percent of their waking hours in just that state.

> Most of a person's everyday life is determined not by their conscious intentions and deliberate choices but by mental processes that are put into motion by features of the environment and that operate outside of conscious awareness and guidance.[40]

For reasons of conservation of mental energy, we are on auto-pilot almost all the time. It's easier on the brain to follow established patterns of thought and behavior as opposed to being in a constant state of considering what to do next.

Fortunately, another state of mind is available to us. This is the Meta-View and it holds within it the solution to our emotional pain, to say nothing of the path to the peak.

You can experience the Meta-View right now by shifting your focus (or attention) from this page to what you are feeling. Locate a feeling in your body and concentrate all your attention on it. You are now in the Meta-View. To begin Lucid Focusing, consciously accept the feeling and then stop thinking. Sit with this inward focus for a few minutes. Observe what happens. Does the feeling change?

When you switch from the absorbed state to the Meta-View and apply Lucid Focusing, something quite extraordinary happens. The feeling begins to dissipate and finally dissolves. And here's the remarkable effect. As the feeling fades away you will enter the Lucid Zone with a pleasurable boost in your General Mood. *And the more you practice this basic technique, the more your General Mood improves.* It was an extraordinary discovery.

In our daily lives we are always susceptible to being triggered by something or someone. Anger, fear, shame, guilt, indignation, jealousy, envy, frustration, feelings of being dissed or rejected, and so on all lie beneath the surface of our conscious minds, waiting to be triggered externally by circumstances or internally by memories or self-talk. The good news is that triggers can be neutralized and essentially wiped clean. The solution lies in the Meta-View and its various applications. From the Meta-View we can make substantial changes that have a lasting effect.

So let's examine why and how Lucid Focusing works.

When you shift your focus from the *stimulus* (or trigger) for the feeling to the *feeling itself*, several things happen concurrently.

Consider the following example. You are chagrined because someone just insulted you. (Chagrin here might mean a combination of feeling hurt, humiliated, frustrated, angry, vengeful, and so on.) The feeling is alloyed with thoughts of what the other person did, how you reacted, how you might have reacted, what you will do to the other person, etc. These thoughts, together with the feeling, are the Knot. And it absorbs everything in your conscious mind including your sense of self and General Mood.

Now you shift all your attention to just what you are feeling. Isolate the feeling in your body and bring the full focus of your consciousness to bear on it. And you accept the feeling and stop thinking. What happens next?

1. Absorption *in* the Knot shifts to focus *on* the feeling *as an object within consciousness*. In other words, the feeling moves from a state of *subjectivity* to one of *objectivity* (so much so that you might form an image of it).

2. Cognition minimizes (if not completely dissolves). Directing consciousness to occupy itself completely with the feeling component of the Knot, removes it from the thinking part.

3. Intentionality shifts. Because you are no longer focused on thinking about the insult, the "aboutness" shifts from the *situation* (that triggered the knot) to the *feeling in the raw*. In other words, your consciousness is now entirely *about* the feeling it is focused on.

4. With "aboutness" shifted away from the situation, the triggered feeling (chagrin) no longer has a stimulus. In other words, because you are focused

on the feeling, you are no longer thinking about what happened, and therefore the triggered feeling has to dissolve. (And it takes any remaining resistance with it as well.)

5. And (if I am right about this part) the feeling receives the acknowledgement from the higher brain centers it seeks and can dissipate.

This dynamic of shifts all occurring more or less simultaneously dismantles the structure of the Knot which keeps the feeling active. And the feeling simply goes away. This is Lucid Focusing.

Here's another personal anecdote:

I had a conflict with my partner. We were collaborating on ghostwriting a client's autobiography and a dispute arose about our different styles of writing. He wanted a more jaunty, popular style and I was invested in a more descriptive, fact-of-the-matter treatment. I reacted badly, triggered into a deep state of resentment fired up by my convictions and self-righteousness. I went for a walk while the Knot played out in graphic painful detail in my mind. I really didn't like being gripped by the inner conflict. "How do I get out of this?" I asked myself. And then I remembered: it's just a Knot. And just then, I was no longer absorbed in it; I was observing it from a slight remove. And almost immediately, it blew apart. That's how it seemed. And for a brief moment I could see pieces of the shrapnel, like bits of cogs and gears, the edges of my ego. And suddenly it all became clear. I remembered that the project was my partner's; I was really only a hired hand. Wasn't it his right to direct the structure and the flow? I had to admit that I was out of place. Writer's ego. I called my partner and it was all straightened out. This is the power of the Meta-View and Lucid Focusing: stepping out of the absorption and focusing on the inner theatre is the first step in changing it (if you want to).

With this knowledge and a little practice, you need never be at the effect of your emotions ever again.

PRACTICE

Chapter 10

The Basic Exercise

Lucid focusing is used to dissolve painful feelings and unwanted cravings as well as a regular practice (focused on any feeling) to produce the pleasurable Moods of the Lucid Zone.

Lucid Focusing: The Basic Technique
- A. Consciously relax your body.
- B. Take a deep breath.
- C. Focus all your attention on a feeling, mood, or craving.
- D. Accept the feeling.
  (Say to yourself, "I accept how I feel.")
- E. Stop thinking.
- F. Keep focusing on the feeling until it changes into something else.

How long? The simple answer is until you notice the dissolution of the feeling or craving and the change in your General Mood. It shouldn't take more than twenty minutes. You can practice Lucid Focusing sitting down, walking around (preferably in a quiet area such as the woods) and with eyes open or shut. Continued practice will produce the desired change in about five minutes or less.

When you become proficient at this simple technique, this is most of what you will have to do. As I mentioned above, the more you focus on what you are feeling, the higher your General Mood rises toward contentment and even joy. It's probably the result of increased serotonin levels, stimulated by the focus on your feelings.

When you experience an especially strong feeling (or Knot), such as anger, fear or shame, you may need to do something else. The Knot and its absorption may be so strong that you find you cannot focus on the feeling and stop your thoughts. The following are some additional aids to help you.

Variations (useful tips):

G. To stop thinking. You will become more adept at this the more you practice it. Of course, implicit in the direction to "focus all your attention on the feeling," is the cessation of thought. But thinking is a persistent mechanism. In the beginning, if you have trouble dissolving your thought processes, try commanding yourself to "Think!" Counter-intuitively, this command will stop the flow of thoughts.

H. Breathe into the feeling (or craving). Visualize your breath flowing into the area of your body where the feeling is located.

I. Point to the location of the feeling in your body. Place your finger on your body at the place where the feeling is felt.

J. Focus with visualization. Imagine that the feeling has a shape and a hue. First change the color. If your anger appears as a black blob with red streaks of lightning, change the black to pink and the lightning bolts to purple fireworks. Second, change the feeling's shape. Expand or shrink the blob or turn it into a completely different shape. These techniques will automatically put you in the Meta-View.

K. Write it down. Name the feeling or craving and write it down, perhaps in a regularly maintained journal. Writing it down serves to objectify it (the Meta-View) in another way than simply focusing on it.

L. Read some of this book. Open it to a random page and begin reading or find a section that deals directly with your current situation. If nothing else, it will take your mind off the intentional part, delay acting on a craving, or allow the mind to shift in another direction.

M. A note on Acceptance.

Acceptance is different from surrender. In surrendering to our feelings, we only increase the absorption. Accepting them preserves the subject/object relationship with them. Accepting them infers that your core sense of self is choosing or willing to allow them full expression while keeping them somewhat removed from a state of full absorption.

> Acceptance is the ability to allow the experience to be as it is in the present moment, to accept pleasant and unpleasant experiences without seeking to hold back the former or reject the latter. According to several authors, emotional suffering results much more from the non-acceptance of the emotion than from the emotion itself. Moreover, change is only possible when the individual has recognized and accepted the emotional distress he feels.[41]

You could say to yourself: "Okay, this is how it is. This is my life at this moment. I accept the situation. I can handle this. It is okay. And the way I feel is also okay. I accept it. It will change soon and I will be back to my old self, if not feeling a whole lot better."

Daily Practice

Make a practice of noting how you feel throughout the day. At least once a day, write down everything you feel. Take five or ten minutes and make a list. The following is one of mine:

<u>Tues. Noon.</u>

Bored
Anxious
Frustrated
Chomping at the bit
Hopeful
Excited
Gnarly
More centered (now)

As you can see, simply writing them down can change how you feel. Observing what you are feeling is the Meta-View. At first, the way you feel may not modulate from the negative to the positive. But eventually it will. The practice will serve as a reminder that feelings are transitory, arbitrary, and contingent—and change when they are observed with Lucid Focusing. Sometimes you may not be able to label what you feel. Feel free to invent a name.

Chapter 11

In the pursuit of learning, everyday something is acquired.
In the pursuit of the Way, everyday something is dropped.

~ Lao-tzu

Advanced Exercises

1. Dissolving Shame

The chapter on shame (7) explored its origin and its structure. The following method will dissolve or transcend your shame file and you will be free of this particular conflict with yourself.

The exercise here is to trace your shame chains backward in time, as I did in the kitchen, and see how far back you can go. When you arrive at the earliest one you can remember, sit with the experience and flesh it out as much as you can. Try to fully feel what you felt at the time. Replay what happened. Take as much time as you need.

The next step is to write about it. Put it all down. I would also suggest writing about the one incident in the chain that had the most impact on you. The one you would least like to talk about. Writing about past experiences serves to make them more fully conscious and less repulsive. Any defenses you may have about such experiences begin to wither away and dissolve. The experience no longer has the same hold on you and the other later memories will wither in response. You have accessed your shame structure (those chains) and disabled it.

The next step would be to tell someone about it or let them read what you have written. In this way, you bring it all into the social sphere which is what the defenses are all about—keeping your shame hidden from other people. The object is to dissolve any resistance to full disclosure.

In addition to the exercise above, simply make a list of everything you are ashamed of. Categories include sex, your body, your social status, what you have done in the past, those evil thoughts, those nasty habits, your flaws, the core feeling of inadequacy (the hole in the soul), and others you might have. Give it time. You might find that you add to the list over several days as new insights occur.

To flesh out the structure of shame in your psyche, ask yourself the following questions for each item in the list:

Is it rational? Is it right?

Would it be shameful in another culture?

What or who is the authority that says this is shameful (tradition, religion, parents, teachers, etc.)?

Ask yourself if you are free to reveal feelings of sadness, fear, shame, failure, or weakness to others. Ask yourself how much you seek the approval of others and avoid their disapproval or rejection.

When the list feels complete, ask yourself if there is any *good* reason to be ashamed of any of it.

Okay, perhaps you have done some extremely bad things, especially to other people. Several issues converge here and they can all be true at the same time. The first is that what you did was wrong, dreadful. The second is that you probably couldn't have done anything different (see the next exercise). The third is that lugging around that millstone of shame will impede your progress toward compassion and turning your life around. When you think about it, feeling ashamed of something you have done is a self-affirming mental function. It's the last ditch effort of the ego to hold on to a smidgeon of self-respect. "Only a basically good person would feel shame about this; a bad person would feel no shame whatsoever." (It can get kind of dark in the cellar of the soul.) In any case, holding on to any kind of shame will stand in the way of any kind of redemption. The best you can do is to make some kind of compensation to the person you wronged (if that is possible) and resolve to move your life in the right direction.

We all need to be clear of this debilitating emotion, no matter what we have done in the past.

After I had written about my self-exploration at the kitchen table, many experiences of shame popped into memory, some of them excruciating, painful, gut-wrenching. The thought that I was obligated to write about them in the interests of candor immediately met with an overwhelming resistance. The structure of shame is cemented with conviction; we believe in the moral justification of the shame. We assume that revelation of the shameful thing will be met with disapproval, rejection, possibly even social exile. However, I immediately recognized that this resistance was the charge that held the shame file in place. And I knew that the only way to neutralize the resistance was to step through it by going public. This shift in consciousness had a profound effect. In a few moments, the charge dissipated and I actually found the whole scenario highly amusing. Funny! Later I was able to tell people about my old shame files matter-of-factly, completely free of any resistance.

Neutralizing the "big one" can be cathartic. For me, it had the effect of placing all the other shame files in relief, recognizing the structure and then seeing the humor.

If, after doing this exercise, you found the humor about your whole shame universe, you probably don't have to do anything else. You are free of it. But if it makes you feel better, or as an exercise in completion, put a match to the list and watch it burn away in the kitchen sink.

The takeaway is that once you have opened your shame file, seen its structure, and experienced the withering if not the dissolution of some discomforting memories, every time one of them resurfaces, you will be able to dismiss it with relative ease. And that, by itself, will have a liberating effect on you.

2. **Meditation on Determinism**

Most philosophers in the realist school accept that human beings have no free will. Many add that we also need to subscribe to free will in order to maintain social order, a moral framework, and a viable justice system. That was the position of the Nobel laureate physicist Stephen Hawking. It's a paradox, of course, and one that contributes to our Cosmic Predicament.

The vast majority of cognitive psychologists believe that human behavior is entirely determined by the fundamental laws of the physical world. More than forty years ago, the American psychologist Benjamin Libet demonstrated that all our conscious decisions are prefigured by electrical activity in the nervous system, that the decision to act in a certain way has already been made before we consciously decide.[42] The cognitive psychologist, Lawrence Barsalou, also wrote that the "illusion of free will" originates in the substrates of the nervous system.[43]

Our "automaticity" (Chapter 9) becomes more comprehensible when we see that it is simply the deterministic stream flowing through human life. One thing after another, almost completely unconsciously.

Willing something *freely* would be to decide in a vacuum, without any prior causes or influences in place, which is clearly unavailable to us.

Some philosophers are of the opinion that we shouldn't tell people they don't have free will because it will lead to the breakdown of social order. Indeed, experimental research in the lab demonstrates that people who come to believe there is no free will "are more likely to behave immorally [and] they stop seeing themselves as blameworthy for their actions."[44] On the other hand, where subjects in a research setting might be induced to cheat on an exam or steal small sums of money, in the real world, they might not be so inclined even when they no longer believe in free will. They would still come up against their internalized moral framework (if not the consequences of getting caught). If free will is seen to be an illusion, the moral constraints against cheating and stealing are not.

Above I alluded to the fact that the deterministic stream is *almost* completely unconscious. The Meta-View is a mental shift out of the stream where elements of the stream can now be considered. The Meta-View has the appearance of a mental state prefiguring free will because it is an intervention in the chain of automatic behaviors. Feeling anxiety, I head toward the liquor store. Then I realise the Knot I'm in. So I stop, take a deep breath, stop thinking, accept the feeling and focus all my attention on it. The anxiety goes away and I am feeling better, having achieved a Lucid Zone pleasurable mood.   I have interrupted my automatic responses. Nevertheless, it's all still deterministic; the chains of cause and effect have simply shifted "above" the usual stream on autopilot to chart a different flight plan. In the language of Normal Waking Reality, it is a decision, an act of will, but one that has not been made *freely*, that is, without prior influence or cause. Stepping into the Meta-View pauses the stream for a moment, allowing you to step back and analyze options. That's perhaps the closest we will get to free will.

But this is the main point: If it's all deterministic then you really couldn't have done anything other than what you did—ever. That immediately brings up a hornet's nest of responses including the fear that the social fabric is at risk. It seems to make perfect sense, but it must be tempered by the paradoxical onus of responsibility. You did it; you couldn't help it; but you're still responsible. It's holding two seemingly contradictory thoughts at the same time, bringing ethics to bear on predetermined behavior.

If you resist this notion (and that's understandable), try to prove that you could have done *anything* differently. It's not possible.

This has two important implications for our purposes here. The first is that our responsibility for past acts means we should attempt to right the wrongs we have committed. Where possible we can seek out those we have wronged and compensate them, or at least sincerely apologize to them. The second is that we can free our minds of all the guilt and shame for what we have done. We can wipe the slate clean.

The exercise here is to make a list of everything that comes up when you think about your past bad behavior. (The guilty list may be quite different from the shameful list in the previous exercise.) Then meditate on the fact that you are not at fault for anything you did. When the guilt comes up, bring Lucid Focusing to bear on the feeling until it dissolves for good.

Obviously this does not liberate you to do harm in the future. It is only about freeing you from remaining mired in your file of misdeeds. You can absolve all of your past behavior, but none of the future.

If by now you have experienced the higher moods of the Lucid Zone, you would know that at that level doing something hurtful to someone else is simply impossible. You are at ease with the world, empathetic if not somewhat compassionate, and ready to play. And if you have neutralized your shame and guilt, nobody will be able to trigger your defenses. Other people are simply opportunities to play.

3. Dissolving Triggers

In the movie *Goodfellas*, there is a memorable bar scene where Billy Batts (played by Frank Vincent) is needling Tommy DeVito (Joe Pesci) about having been a shoe-shine boy when he was younger. DeVito (now a gangster with a lot of clout) is not amused, commenting that there are a lot of people within earshot. Batts apologizes and things calm down. For a moment. After a brief lull, Batts suddenly yells, "Now go home and get your fuckin' shine box!" DeVito explodes in rage, leaves the bar and returns when all the customers are gone. Sneaking up behind Batts, he proceeds to lay a spectacular beating on him (with assistance from Robert De Niro) and then shoots him in his open foul mouth.

Tetchy!

The scene illustrates the potential of the shame file to open with a vengeance. All it needs is an appropriate trigger. Everyone has a personal file created when we were very young and filled in as we grew into adulthood. We live out our lives ever susceptible to being triggered by the others around us.

Of course it could be said that all our emotions are the products of various triggers. What we want to neutralize are the negative ones: shame, anger, fear, sadness, desperation, and so on. We could simply apply Lucid

Focusing to the negative responses as they arise, but that may not dissolve the internal trigger mechanism itself.

The first step is to see the structure. The trigger structure is composed of three basic elements: determinism (one thing after another), absorption (automaticity), and the shame file. Recognizing the structure takes us out of our daily absorption in our stream of experience and behavior. Absorption is akin to being engrossed in a movie. We become so involved in the screen story that we may forget that we are sitting in a theatre. This is a different sort of involvement with the film that a film student may have. The film student may be following the movement of the camera while the plot unfolds. This is akin to observation from the Meta-View, only we can't make changes to the movie while we can do so when observing what goes on in our heads. In the absorbed state, a slight from someone immediately triggers the shame file and a feeling that attempts to protect the self within the social context. Feeling shame, we then feel fear, anger, and so on and then react with either a backlash or a descent into demoralization. Striking back may trigger the other's shame file and the interaction becomes a chain reaction of triggered mutual abuse. Reflecting back on the interaction from a calmer state of mind, we may not fully understand what had happened.

Once you recognize the trigger structure, the second step is to respond to a trigger in a different way that stops the chain reaction before it happens. You can, for instance, react with curiosity, or as a chance to play, commiserate or inform. If you have done the exercise on shame above, you may have dissolved much if not all of your shame file and are no longer fazed by insults. To get at the other triggers, do the following.

Begin by making a list of everything that might trigger a negative reaction, for instance, what makes you angry; what scares you; what brings up resentment; and so on. Imagine each situation and allow the resulting feeling to come up fully. Then use Lucid Focusing to neutralize the feeling. The more you do this, the more you will unlink yourself from the Automaticity (Chapter 9) of your experience with the world. Or at least change it from negative to positive.

You will arrive at a point where you welcome disrespect from others, as a chance to play, simply ignore, laugh or instruct. As Michelle Obama insightfully said, "When they go low, we go high."

When you arrive at a point of self-possession in the trenches of human interaction, you will likely see the cosmic joke in taking what others say about you seriously.

The test for trigger and shame dissolution is to imagine someone attempting to trigger your shame by calling you a nasty name. This could be something like "loser," "wimp," an ethnic slur, a slur on your body ("fatso") or intelligence ("idiot"), or any other disparaging epithet that you might think of. When the insult passes cleanly through your consciousness without stirring up any dust, you've arrived at your trigger- and shame-free place. You might see an opportunity to turn the situation into play. Or you might see the opportunity to educate the other person: "You know, I don't react to insults anymore; I've cleared my mind of them and you can too. Would you like me to show you how?" Or you might throw your head back in raucous laughter. Having seen the shame structure and dissolved it, you now recognize the absurdity of the entire enterprise.

4. The no purpose, no meaning, no explanation meditation

This one addresses our existential angst (and the Cosmic Predicament). The truth is we are all isolated units floating on a rock through space with no discernible starting point or destination, no meaning or purpose (in the cosmic sense), no explanation and no way out except death. That's the rub.

When you become absorbed by this thought, it changes things. The first thing it does is produce some sort of feeling response. The feeling could be anxiety, fear, disappointment, despair, emptiness, or a sense of eeriness. That is why we don't dwell on it.

So what is the point? Well, the silver lining in this exercise is that if you objectify the feeling with Lucid Focusing, it will dissolve like all the others and you will be free of it.

Try it. Sink into the following thought:

"There is no meaning to life, no purpose,
and no explanation."

Then notice how you feel.

Let the feeling become fully conscious. Focus all your attention on the feeling. Notice if the feeling has a shape and/or a hue.

What happens? The feeling should dissolve away leaving you in a rather novel and pleasant General Mood. That's the real salvation—the confluence of moods and affects at the higher levels: contentment, even joy, connectedness, compassion, and an elevated sense of whimsy—in spite of everything.

It is here that the cosmic joke resonates most strongly. When meaning, purpose and explanation are seen to have no significance, at least in the cosmic sense (the meaning of life), our agonizing over finding the answer will be seen as a colossal joke.

I want to pause here to emphasize a point. Those who "get it" about this life understand that every human being is dignified by the Cosmic Predicament. We all just popped into this existence. Over time we developed a sense of self. This naked sense at the core of our experience is what unites us all. This experience is the same for everyone. The previous two sentences could be the entire cosmology of a new religion. Those who get it know that all religious cosmologies are fables. They are stories we tell ourselves to resolve the issues of separateness, death, purpose and meaning, which are all irresolvable. That's just the way it is. The only way out is to arrive at a point where you no longer care about it (or find it extraordinarily funny). Neutralize the fear (of uncertainty) and what does the Cosmic Predicament matter anymore? What is left is to join hands and help each other out.   That seems to be part of what our religions have aimed to do.

5. The Void

The Void is a particularly uncomfortable place to be. On the other hand, it intrigues me. What is it all about? I describe my own particular Void as a combination of meaninglessness, purposelessness, hopelessness, together with a complete lack of interest in anything. It is a place of abject emptiness, a conscious wasteland, desolate, bleak, barren, and dismal. The Void is closer to an all-encompassing mood rather than a reactive feeling. It just emerges within consciousness without any discernible stimulus. Everything inside me crashes into the abyss.

Now consider the following constellation of attitudes: "powerlessness (futility), meaninglessness (emptiness), and nonfulfillment (frustration)."[45] In a comprehensive paper on the evolution of the self, the social psychologist, Roy Baumeister, wrote that this melange of mental states became more prevalent in 20th century literature as social alienation increased. Explaining the Void as a visceral relic of our alienation seems appropriate to me. And it means that the feeling is probably experienced by most people at one time or another. Fortunately, there is a remedy for the feeling that at least diminishes its effect on us.

One would think that applying Lucid Focusing to the feeling should work. However, in the beginning, this method did not work very well for me. It was as though the qualities of the Void followed me into the Meta-View and sapped my will to focus on it. What worked best was simply accepting it, surrendering to it and allowing it to play itself out. The Void does not come up much these days and when it does, it is much less overwhelming and Lucid Focusing takes care of it fairly quickly.

Tear this page out (or copy it) and carry this message with you. The next time you fall into the Void, pull it out and read it.

> You are not alone in this feeling. It happens
> to most everyone.   It is a by-product of our
> alienation. You don't have to follow your
> urge to medicate it (tobacco, alcohol, drugs,
> or sweets). You can try to dissolve it with
> Lucid Focusing. If that doesn't work, you
> can surrender to it. Say to yourself, "This is
> the way life is right now and I can handle it.
> I accept it for what it is." Try this simple
> exercise before you deal with it in any other
> way. If only to see what happens.

6. The Death Meditation

Death is part of our existential pain, but deserves a section all of its own. See if you can bring your fear of death centre stage. Stay with it as long as you can (perhaps ten minutes or so) and allow any attending images to do their own thing. Then apply Lucid Focusing. Focus completely on whatever you are feeling. After the feelings dissipate you will never again feel the same about death. It just won't bother you much anymore. And, as always, you get the joke.

Death becomes just an event in one's life, a datum, without much significance. It does not trigger any response (certainly not a negative one).

7. It's all about Love and Play

I once had two friends, a woman and her eleven-year-old daughter. Whenever we got together, the daughter and I would spontaneously leap into some sort of play. One day we were dancing with our hands over the table and I had the distinct revelation that this is what it is all about: play and love, love and play. Nothing else really mattered that much. So, for me life became injecting some play into every human encounter, friend and stranger.

See how much you agree with the above. See how much play you can create with others. The love will come along shortly.

All the intellectualizations lead here. Figuring it out is not the same as living it.

8. Do I care?

Ask yourself the following question: Do I care about myself?

Wait for the answer.

How does the answer make you feel?

Focus on the feeling without thinking about it. What happens to the feeling?

I was stoned one day, walking the tree-lined street toward home, and the question popped into mind. And I didn't have a ready answer. *Did* I care about myself? And then I saw in relief the extent of the time and effort I spent questioning everything. And I realized that I must really care about something and that caring was at the heart of my soul. I could answer, "Yes, I care about myself."

Complete the following sentence: I must really care about myself because I spend so much time (thinking, worrying, planning, living in fear, living in conflict, medicating myself, etc.) _________________.

Do this exercise with some regularity (say, once a week) until you see the humor.

9. Lucid Thinking

In the following list, check off all the ones that you believe in.

God

Cosmic consciousness (or panpsychism)

Angels

Heaven

Reincarnation

The Law of Attraction (the idea that the mind can attract anything by merely willing it)

Quantum mysticism (the idea that quantum physics proves cosmic consciousness)

Karma (the idea that justice is meted out by a cosmic algorithm)

Soul (an indwelling entity that survives bodily death)

Astrology

ESP

UFOs

For each one you checked, ask yourself the following questions and write down your answers.

1. Why do I believe this?
2. What does believing this resolve or satisfy in my life?
3. How does my belief relate to the unanswered questions of the Cosmic Predicament?
4. How would I feel if this belief was proved beyond doubt to be false?

It is important to spend time on #4. If you can successfully bring up what you would feel upon realizing that the belief is false, you can now apply Lucid Focusing to the feeling until it dissolves and you enter the Lucid Zone. Then it just doesn't matter anymore.

This exercise takes some courage, so congratulate yourself.

10.   Getting the Cosmic Joke

To fully appreciate the following quotations, go online, search for the audio file of Alan Watts laughing and play it while you read them.

When a foolish man hears of the Tao,

He laughs out loud.

If he didn't laugh

It wouldn't be the Tao.

~ Lao Tzu, *Tao Te Ching*

If I could tell you what it meant, there would be no point in dancing it.

~ Isadora Duncan

Followers of the Way, don't take the Buddha to be some sort of ultimate goal. In my view he's more like the hole in a privy.

~ Lin-chi, *Zen Teachings*

"Sometimes we can become so enamored of our ideas that we project them onto the world, mistaking our own mode of thought for something as grand as 'God's plan.'"[46]

"Our minds may be designed to detect meaning, whether or not there is any to be found."[47]

"The art inspired by God's laughter does not propagate, but rather contradicts, ideological certitudes. Like Penelope, it undoes each night the tapestry that theologians, philosophers, and learned men wove the day before."[48]

"A person might be most ready to laugh when every pretense about reality finally vanishes."[49]

"No peace is possible between the novelist and the *agelaste* [someone who never laughs]. Never having heard God's laughter, the *agelastes* are convinced that the truth is obvious, that all men necessarily think the same thing, and that they are themselves exactly what they think they are. But it is precisely in losing the certainty of truth and the unanimous agreement of others that man becomes an individual."[50]

"We all know that in things as they are, in the universe as it is, in man's nature as *it* is, there is a principle that renders our every move, our every word, inadequate, undercuttable, subject to corrective crosslights at least some of which are beyond our vision."[51]

"Hostages of the crypto-theological belief that human beings are in some sense a uniquely important part of the world, we will continue to try to impose our illusions on it until the world proves we are wrong."[52]

"If we were to experience the world exactly as it is, we'd be too depressed to get out of bed in the morning. But if we were to experience the world exactly as we want it to be, we'd be too deluded to find our slippers."[53]

"If anybody says he can think about quantum theory *without* getting giddy, it merely shows that he hasn't understood the first thing about it!"[54]

"It is not merely that each thing means something, but that each thing means almost anything."[55]

"We seem incapable of talking about the vacuum for very long without ascribing qualities to it or discovering things in it."[56]

"As soon as you have made a thought, laugh at it."

~ Lao Tzu, *Tao Te Ching*

"A-wop-bop-a-loo-mop-a-lop-bam-boom!"

~ Little Richard, "Tutti Frutti"

Chapter 12

"Passion destroys passion;
we want what puts an end to wanting what we want."
~ John Fowles, *The Aristos*

Craving

This is the hard part.

Among all the actors in the inner theatre, cravings are perhaps the most compelling and the most difficult to deal with on the path to enlightenment. In Chapter 8 I separated out our unwanted cravings from the others because they are most probably the ones that are unhealthy, risky and addictive. We would rather not be slaves to them, but we are not strong or "willful" enough to resist them.

If you have been practicing Lucid Focusing you will have noticed that the elevated moods of the Lucid Zone feel much different than the satisfaction of any craving. Both are pleasurable, but distinctly different. It is as though pleasure is experienced on two parallel tracks. On the one track is the range of elevated moods, such as contentment, joy, and euphoria and on the other, the buzz, the kick, the rush. If you had to choose one track over the other, which one would it be? Once experienced, the buzz becomes simply irresistible.

Whether the activity is drugs (tobacco, alcohol, cannabis, and so on), gambling, shopping, video games, or (fill in the blanks), the buzz is a stronger pull than contentment or equanimity. ("Euphoria" might appear to straddle both tracks, but the euphoria experienced in the higher stages of mindfulness is a much different feeling than that experienced from smoking cannabis, snorting cocaine or having an orgasm. It's that word problem again.) If we had to choose, the buzz is always the stronger candidate. Until we see different.

The two pleasure tracks have been verified by neural science. Robert Lustig is a professor of pediatrics at the University of California and the author of the book *The Hacking of the American Mind*. The book exposes how various industries (such as food and gambling) manipulate our brain chemistry to induce us to consume their products. Lustig introduces us to a fascinating but relatively unknown property of our neurology. Our brains deliver gratification along two separate neural pathways, one which produces the neurotransmitter serotonin and the other, dopamine. (Lustig has defined a neurotransmitter as "a biochemical manufactured in the brain that drives feelings and emotions."[57]) Serotonin stimulates the feelings or moods associated with the first track. Dopamine is the reward chemical; it produces the buzz or the rush. It's what makes the lab rats press the cocaine lever again and again. And it's what makes the rest of us gamble or shop our money away, eat sweets, salt and fat, play video games, smoke, drink and snort.

Let's refer to the two pleasure tracks as the Lucid Zone and the Buzz Zone. But feel free to give them your own names. The point is to highlight and distinguish the two states of mind so they may be compared. After that, it inevitably becomes a matter of choice.

In my experience, each zone has a distinctive shape and feel.

The Buzz Zone is essentially cyclical. A craving leads to some sort of indulgence that produces a dopamine buzz which lasts for a while and then descends into a hangover which makes it more likely you will indulge again. The buzz zone is a roller coaster of dramatic ups and downs. We may even romanticize the indulgent lifestyle. My heroes were Rimbaud, Baudelaire, Huxley, and so on, and in a lesser way, Leary and even Bukowski: the artists who stimulated their visions with various intoxicants. I came to *identify* with them. The point here is only to see the structure of reinforcement, the deterministic stream, the absorption in our habitual behavior, and the ways in which we justify self-sabotaging activities.

If you are indulging regularly, you are pretty much in the Buzz Zone all the time.

If we look deeper, we may find that each craving was precipitated by some sort of negative feeling or mood.

When we experience feelings of loneliness, boredom, anger, fear and general malaise we immediately medicate them without giving it much thought.

And if we look even deeper, we may find something more primordial. Stephen Batchelor was a Buddhist monk for several years and wrote *Buddhism Without Beliefs* which became a bestseller. The book is a relatively modest size (less than 130 pages) but succeeds in demystifying much of what has accrued to Buddha's teachings as they moved through history and cultures. Once the teachings have been stripped down to their essentials, Batchelor writes, they reveal a practical method for alleviating human existential pain, but without any mystical insight. "The Buddha was not a mystic," Batchelor wrote. He simply "discovered complete freedom of heart and mind from the compulsions of craving."[58] (Buddha called this freedom "the taste of the *dharma*."[59]) Of all the examples of thought-provoking prose in the book (of which there are many), one sentence in particular stuck out and gave me pause: *"Anguish emerges from craving for life to be other than it is."*[60]

Ponder that for a moment. Elsewhere he writes, "This craving to be otherwise, to be elsewhere, permeates the body, feelings, perceptions, will—consciousness itself. It is like the background radiation from the big bang of birth, the aftershock of having erupted into existence."[61] Craving burns at the center of the hole in the soul, the aching need for something more, something different, and is the pulse of our Cosmic Predicament.

We may not be able to fully extinguish the core visceral craving; it might have had some sort of primitive survival value. Being at peace with the world may have made one easy prey. Obviously, we weren't meant to be too comfortable here. The takeaway is that *you are not at fault for any of it*, not the cravings nor the addictions that result. Blame the automatic stream propelling you through life. That can set the stage for inserting into your stream alternative thoughts and behaviors.

In contrast to the Buzz Zone, the Lucid Zone is grounded and expansive. It opens with equanimity and contentment and rises through joy, euphoria and rapture, to the edges of *kensho* (see Chapter 4). Its elevated moods are also attended by connection (or communion), compassion and a renewed sense of humor, and all its flavours rise and fall in intensity. The Lucid Zone is free of craving, there is no hangover, and it can easily be produced by Lucid Focusing (mindfulness).

So how do we extinguish our unwanted cravings?

First a personal anecdote:

I was walking to the store on a *Jones* to buy a cigar and some wine. Then, out of the blue, the thought surfaced to shift into Meta-View, if only to see what happens. I decided to try it, but as soon as I did there was a bump of resistance. It was as though Mr. Jones was making one final appeal. The "bump" (as I call it) is an interesting mental event. In order to come to grips with it, let's revisit two previously explored items: determinism and absorption. The first refers to the mechanistic stream of cause and effect that drives the universe, including us. The second refers to the relationship between human consciousness and the deterministic stream. It is thought that we spend 95% of our lives in a state akin to auto-pilot. Our consciousness is absorbed in the stream of events that we follow without much thinking about it. And much of the stream is driven by the force of our cravings. We get hungry and we eat. We feel stress and we medicate ourselves with some sort of substance. It's all so *automatic*. In the case of our self-sabotaging indulgences, any thoughts about not indulging are met by the bump. If the deterministic stream is the path of least resistance, the bump is the friction produced by changing directions, even the *intention* to change directions. The bump is the critical choice point. For about five seconds, it seems insurmountable. And it often wins the day, keeping me on my original path. It is a cog in the machinery of my auto-pilot. I managed to get over this particular bump relatively quickly and focus all my attention on the cravings. And they began to shift and weaken and finally dissolve. I was back in the Lucid Zone. I had no desire to smoke or drink and I was enjoying how I felt.

The important question here is what caused that thought to come out of the blue? And can I program myself such that the thought arises in response to every urge to consume something?

We know that unnatural cravings eventually dissipate simply by not indulging them. People who have quit smoking, for instance, report that after the withdrawal symptoms have died away, they arrive at a point where the very thought of lighting up again makes them queasy. Further, by now you may easily think that Lucid Focusing on a craving will dissolve it. And it does. On paper, it all looks so easy. In one's consciousness it's much more complicated. Remember we are almost always on auto-pilot. What is needed is some sort of intervention between a sudden craving and its indulgence. If we could insert a pause whenever we experience a craving, and then shift to the Meta-View and focus on the craving, the craving will eventually dissolve. It sounds good in theory, but the pull of the craving may hijack any attempts to not satisfy it.

One answer is nurturing your resolve. Resolve is defined as "firmness of purpose; determination." Most of us have resolved to do things in our lives and many of those resolutions remain unfulfilled. Nevertheless, at the time we resolve to do something, it is heartfelt, sincere, and feels certain. Inevitably we fall back into the deterministic stream and it's the same old one thing after another. We have to nurture our resolve on a continuing basis. Stephen Batchelor devoted an entire chapter of *Buddhism Without Beliefs* to the subject. "*Dharma* practice is founded on resolve," he wrote. "This is not an emotional conversion, a devastating realization of the error of our ways, a desperate urge to be good, but an ongoing, heartfelt reflection on priorities, values, and purpose. We need to keep taking stock of our life in an unemotional, uncompromising way."[62]

To strengthen your resolve, do the following:

1. Start every day with a Lucid Focusing session.
2. Place Sticky Note reminders where you spend the most time in your home.
3. Post a large sign in your home titled The Lucid Zone.
4. Schedule times for Lucid Focusing and program pings on your cell phone to remind you.
5. Commit to inserting a pause immediately after you experience an unwanted craving.

Putting all this together, the following is the formula for dissolving unwanted cravings.

The first step is to reify the difference between the Lucid Zone and the Buzz Zone. Visualize them. Give each one a shape and a hue and perhaps a tone. What do you think about them? How does each one feel? When the zones become distinct mental objects, they produce the inescapable element of choice. And you may see that the choice between them isn't a utilitarian one or a moral one, or an issue about strength of character. The choice is a *spiritual* one. It is about the quality of your inner space, the purity of your consciousness, the essence of your soul. You may see that the Lucid Zone is more "authentic," natural or soulful and that the Buzz Zone is artificial, contaminated, and compulsive. The more you nurture the Lucid Zone (by Lucid Focusing), the more you will want it to be a frequent state if not a permanent one. And gradually you will drift toward the Lucid Zone in your own time.

When you do enter the Meta-View in response to a craving, do the following:

1. Relax the body.
2. Focus on the craving and breathe into it.
3. Stop thinking.
4. Maintain your focusing through the "bump."
5. Commit to enduring some measure of discomfort.
6. Keep focused; the craving will begin to dissolve in a very short time.
7. When you reach equanimity, say to yourself: "Ahhh, I'm back in the Lucid Zone."

8. Now focus on how you are feeling to reach even higher mood levels.

Don't worry too much if there are setbacks. This process can take some time. Eventually, you will be free of all your unwanted cravings.

The key to this entire book is that the more often you shift into the Meta-View and Lucid Focusing, the more your General Mood improves. And the more your General Mood improves, the more it can seem like an enlightened state of mind.

Chapter 13

True enlightenment comes when we get the joke, dump the baggage, and get *loose*.

True Enlightenment

We are born into a Cosmic Predicament....

> Marooned on an island in a sea of stars,
> with no good answers to the most pressing
> questions....

> > What is going on?
> > How do I make sense of this?
> > What does it all mean?
> > Who am I?
> > Why?

> > Why *me*?

In a way, it's a setup: the mind is designed to *construe* things, but at both poles of the Predicament, the universe and the mind itself, it just may be unconstruable.

From the earliest times we have created stories that serve to explain things, but since the great age of the Enlightenment (17th and 18th centuries) they have less and less narrative weight. Science tells us that we are a product of evolution, a construct of biology, experience, and social conditioning; and that the stream of evolution is (arguably) deterministic. Free will is an illusion; it's just one of the stories we tell ourselves.

It's hard to grasp this fully. We become so absorbed in the story of our lives. It's hard to believe that the self we intuit as the object in our sense of self (I really have to put it that way) has no real control over what is happening. Sure, things change; there is a decision to do something different, but nothing would suggest that any of it is directly linked with our sense of self. It looks like it, it feels like it, but that could be an illusion (and probably is).

Our lives would be on continuous autopilot except for one saving grace: the mind's singular ability to shift into the Meta-View. Instead of being swept along in our usual unexamined stream of events, we can rise above it, observe it, and play with it. It's such an important mental event that I wonder why it isn't common knowledge. We all do it, like when we are asked how we are feeling or what we are thinking, but most people may not be aware that what they just did has a name.

The Meta-View is important because it sets the stage for several significant mental operations. From here we can focus on a particular element (such as a feeling, the breath or a mantra), achieve sustained one-pointedness of mind (without thought), and ascend the levels until we reach the peak (nirvana, samadhi, or moksha). Alternatively, we can take a wider point of view, apply a little thought, and arrive at some valuable insights about ourselves. In addition, we can make some interventions in both the direction of our stream and the imprints we have acquired that drive our habits of thought and behavior. The first operation is mindfulness, the second is introspection, and the third is introspective intervention. Together they provide solutions for resolving the Predicament, the problem of the self, as well as our existential anxiety. After we explore these three Meta-View operations, we'll take a serious look at the Cosmic Joke.

1. Mindfulness: the Lucid Zone and *kensho*

The peak gets all the press, but it isn't the most important aspect in the meditative arc. The peak only lasts a moment. We can't live there and we really wouldn't want to. Where we want to be is a few levels below in the Lucid Zone. The serotonin produced here is experienced as an ascending range of pleasurable moods, an expansive sense of connection, and unselfconscious spontaneity perfectly compatible with everyday life.

Further, in my experience, Lucid Focusing, relative to other forms of mindfulness, seems to stimulate feelings of compassion, as well as an enhanced willingness to play. We may also have more reason to laugh—for no reason at all. The Lucid Zone is the Middle Way between the peak and the stream.

Above the Lucid Zone, but before the peak, we may experience *kensho*-like states similar to my experience in India described in Chapter 4. The key characteristic of these states is that the filters between awareness and the outer world have dissolved. We are no longer involved in the construing process. Gone are cognition, representation, attribution, reification, categorization, and so on. Things just are as they are. There may remain a dim sense of self, but the extended self with all its identity attributions is gone or has at least become unimportant. Here, in this conscious space, the Cosmic Predicament is resolved. When we stop trying to make sense of things, the Predicament ceases to exist.

2. Introspection: Why me?

Our sense of self is a subjective experience without any objective or substantive status. It occupies no specific location in the brain and cannot be isolated for viewing or probing. It is "merely" a brain process. The core sense of self is produced by the neural networks we were born with and the extended self is a product of our experience in the world.

To wit (if not wisdom):

The core self is a *biological* construct; the extended self is a *cultural* construct.

This explains "what" we are. The "why" unfortunately will never be explained to anyone's satisfaction. There is no credible answer that would suggest divine intention or purpose, but the answer embedded in chance, serendipity—fortune—can be a greater miracle. Nearly 14 billion years after the birth of the universe, you and I appeared—without fanfare, without explanation. This occurrence, this confluence of inscrutable events, culminating in a sense of selfhood, is surely the miracle of miracles. The sense of self you have is the only one like it that has ever been or will ever be again in the entire universe.

That's the first insight. If you allow yourself to sink into it, you will have your own Moment of Cosmic Self-Realization (Chapter 1). What feelings come up? Any humor?

When a self "gets it" about itself, pretense drops, the public face cracks up, self-attributes wither, and we are now free to play (without rules). It's just not that serious any more.

The second insight follows from the first.

"Getting it" about ourselves means that we get it about everyone else. Everyone has this same sense of a core self. At the deepest level we are all united by this inescapable fact. Furthermore, we are all in the same boat, unique individuals immersed in the same Cosmic Predicament. Our senses of connection, empathy and compassion are attended by the recognition of the other's *subjectivity* as "same but different"—and worthy of a helping hand.

The enlightened mind identifies *first* with the deepest part of being human, the core sense of self (*before* any other self-attribute such as gender, race, religion, nationality, etc.), and recognizes the connection with everyone else.

3. Intervention: Clearing the Baggage

Perhaps the most significant aspect of the introspective side of the Meta-View is our ability to make interventions in both the deterministic stream and the imprints in our extended selves (the baggage). All the interventions presented in these pages begin with becoming conscious of the contents of the inner theatre and acting on them in specific ways. By itself the Meta-

View is an intervention on the stream and its self-absorption. From "above," the elements of the stream are now merely objects whose habitual "next steps" can be changed or simply ignored. Knots, triggers, and cravings, for instance, wither and dissolve under a sustained view from above. This is true not only in the moment, but also in future episodes. With practice, knots (and the others) automatically "trigger" the shift into the Meta-View and the forging of a more positive response.

The first intervention might be simply inserting a pause before the habitual action occurs. Sometimes consciously accepting either one's internal state or external circumstances is enough to change things. And of course Lucid Focusing is a powerful tool to dissolve negative feelings and lift one's mood into the Lucid Zone. Dissolving the feelings associated with negative self-image, death, determinism, and the Cosmic Predicament liberates us from these concerns.

Perhaps the most dynamic effect of the Meta-View is dissolving the shame file. This powerful exercise was the first one presented in Chapter 11. You may discover, as I did, that getting rid of your shame has an almost immediate liberating effect. After I had brought the shameful stuff into consciousness, ran the scenarios through my mind, wrote about them, and then got to the point of being willing to tell others about them in detail (with some trepidation), the entire repressive structure around them collapsed. I was free of their hold on me. But what happened next was a complete surprise. As soon as I got over the hurdle of self-disclosure, a ripple of humor stirred and promptly broke out into a hearty chuckle. Spontaneously—out of nowhere. It was a Wizard of Oz moment. And in the following days and weeks the dropping of the veil resulted in a palpable lifting of a great weight on my soul. It was as though an internal dam burst, releasing years of pent-up energies, all constrained by the fear of condemnation.

I became free of approval-seeking, disapproval, rejection, self-imposed controls on my behavior in the company of others, the fear of upsetting someone, and being thought of as weird. Am I ridiculous? Yes … and no. I am just a channel for mysterious energies. And I am not at fault for any of it.

4. Getting the Joke

Quantum field theory is a model—a human contrivance. We test our models to find out if they work; but we can never be sure, even for highly predictive models like quantum electrodynamics, to what degree they correspond to "reality." To claim they do is metaphysics. If there were an empirical way to determine ultimate reality, it would be physics, not metaphysics; but it seems there isn't.[63]

That's the Predicament on the subatomic level, but it is analogous to our everyday circumstances. The gap between our *models* (or worldviews) of reality and reality itself is simply unbridgeable—by design. That's the Cosmic Joke, but it's a bit on the wry side of things: unfathomability woven into the very fabric of the world we are trying to understand. The drive to make sense of things in a nonsensical place. Niels Bohr, the quantum pioneer, allowed that quantum theory made him "giddy."[64]

Most quantum physicists today accept the premise of the opening paragraph, that metaphysics does not explain quantum mechanics, but that was not always the case. In the early days, even the luminaries in the field looked to eastern mystical thought to "make sense" of quantum weirdness. According to the physicist Sadri Hassan, "The founders of quantum physics—Niels Bohr, Werner Heisenberg, Wolfgang Pauli, and Erwin Shrödinger—all developed a strong affinity for Eastern theosophy and, regrettably, *tied their science to that mystical viewpoint*."[65] Heisenberg, for instance, following his conversations with the Indian poet

Rabindranath Tagore, said, "Some of the ideas that had seemed so crazy suddenly made *much more sense.*"[66]

The importance of this historical anecdote is that it illustrates the pressing need to understand things even to the extent of grasping at metaphysical straws. It is the same with our own layperson's efforts to make sense of things. That single need, among all the others that motivate us, is the one that can only be satisfied by creating those same metaphysical straws. Otherwise, we are left with uncertainty—unfathomability—at the core of our belief systems. And that is unacceptable to the inquiring mind. All the cosmologies of the world's religions contradict each other and are nevertheless taken very seriously by their respective adherents. That's where the conflicts begin. It's the endless war between competing versions of God.

The gods of course are the supreme authorities. We erect our gods to resolve the Predicament. They provide the meaning, purpose and *answers* we so desperately crave. And even though they vary both across and within cultures and also change through time, the gods remain totems of eternal truths; and of course they also serve the purpose of social control.

The hierarchy of gods and minds is mirrored within the mind itself. The ego controls the impulses of the id at the service of the inner authority of the superego. This arrangement is analogous to the political spectrum which exhibits the extremes of authoritarianism and anarchism, the iron fist and the loose cannon. Democracy occupies the happy middle: freedom of expression with some necessary rules of order. As a nation (or a psyche) moves toward authoritarianism, comedy withers and eventually dies. And that's when the Joke becomes subversive.

It is well known that authoritarians—fascists, dictators—don't appreciate the jokes about them. In fact, they hate them. This fact has motivated various pro-democracy movements to use humor in creative ways to keep in focus the illegitimacy, lack of credibility, and absurdity of various authoritarian regimes. A take on activism, it has been called laughtivism.[67]

On the Web you can find many articles on the authoritarian personality, including the famous book on the subject by Theodor Adorno. The authoritarian profile is characterized by several traits including fear of and resistance to the impulses of the id (especially sexual ones), ambiguity, imaginative or intellectual thought, and the unconventional. It is thought that the authoritarian personality is nurtured in an overly repressive family, mostly by a father who enforces obedience to strict rules with the threat of violence. The authoritarian adult (now in a position of power and able to inflict his own brand of discipline on others) is unable to see anything funny about what he has become. Mockery is seen as an insurgent or iconoclastic impulse aimed at toppling the rigid edifice he has spent a lifetime erecting. To the authoritarian, everything in life is—and should be—deadly serious.

I used to think that becoming the leader of a nation would make one indifferent to any sort of verbal or written diatribe. Such a major accomplishment would either seal up or wash away any psychological vulnerabilities. It would surely be trigger-free. That's what we think. Echoing Sue Erikson Bloland from Chapter 7, we want to believe that enough recognition and admiration will heal us, but they don't. The shame file persists because, for one it has been imprinted and reinforced since childhood, and for two, it remains the motivator—the driver—behind the dictator's epic struggle to seize the reins of power. The fact that it doesn't simply dissolve at the top perhaps makes it that much worse for the despot. The skin is now that much thinner.

By now we have noticed that the authoritarian profile is the antithesis of the Lucid Zone. There is not even a hint of connection or empathy, let alone compassion in the autocrat. Spontaneity has been stifled; play is forbidden; and the belly laugh isn't even a possibility. Instead, what we see is emotional armouring, social alienation (disconnection), and an attitude of righteous superiority. Self-regard is riddled with primordial shame and guilt structured on an error in thinking: "I don't deserve to be loved because my natural impulses (spontaneity) are bad, shameful, dirty."

Dissolving the shame file requires a concerted effort to face it, accept it, see the structure, and eventually let it go. It is intriguing to ponder what would happen to the autocrat who actually managed to purge his soul in this way. Would he come down to earth, serve the people, loosen up?

Would he be able to laugh at himself?

The Joke is woven into the ways we attempt to overturn or compensate for the Predicament:

- Certainty
- Self-importance
- Righteousness
- Superiority
- Pretense
- Entitlement
- Hubris
- Claims of Enlightenment

➢ It is released when we see through them. And then we don't take ourselves so seriously anymore.

To be able to laugh (even guffaw) at the entire arrangement, from the unfathomability of the cosmos, to the serendipity of the self, to the aeonian Predicament that binds them together in a hapless quest for answers, meaning, purpose, or resolution, *is* the answer. That makes it all rather simple, doesn't it? Enlightened maybe?

# # #

The mind is the playground. It's all great fun; if I didn't have these forays into the inner theatre, life would not be as interesting, possibly pointless, certainly boring.

We want to play, not obey.

Putting all this together, we arrive at a level of being, a state of consciousness where most of the baggage is gone, where the self is seen for what it is, and we are connected—and we are *loose*.

One Last Moment

In the opening chapter, I mentioned that I had found only a handful of personal accounts of the Moment of Cosmic Self-Realization. This one is from Stephen Batchelor, the author of *Buddhism Without Beliefs*.

> I was walking through a pine forest, returning to my hut along a narrow path trodden into the steep slope of the hillside. I struggled forward carrying a blue plastic bucket filled with fresh water that I had just collected from a source at the upper end of the valley. I was then suddenly brought to a halt by the upsurge of an overwhelming sense of the sheer mystery of everything. It was as though I were lifted up onto the crest of a shivering wave, which abruptly swelled from the ocean that was life itself. "How is it that people can be unaware of this most obvious question?" I asked myself. "How can anyone pass their life without responding to it?"[68]

Two Koans

We shall not cease from exploration
And the end of all our exploring
Will be to arrive where we started
And know the place for the first time.[69]

The road above
And the road below
Are one…
And this is it![70]

A Few Final Thoughts

"Enlightenment is man's release from his self-incurred tutelage. Tutelage is man's inability to make use of his understanding without direction from another. Self-incurred is this tutelage when its cause lies not in lack of reason but in lack of resolution and courage to use it without direction from another. ***Sapere aude!*** 'Have courage to use your own reason!'- that is the motto of enlightenment."

> ~ Immanuel Kant, *What Is Enlightenment?*

"The dignity of a man lies in his ability to face reality in all its meaninglessness."

> ~ Martin Esslin, *The Theatre of the Absurd*

"Our life is a faint tracing on the surface of mystery."

> ~ Annie Dillard, *Pilgram at Tinker Creek*

"We're all bozos on this bus."   ~ The Firesign Theatre

Acknowledgements

Richard Gutter, for too much that can be adequately listed. Richard "got it" very early in his life and has been a constant source of insight, valuable critique, and unconditional support.

John Ince, for his insightful conversations, unconditional support, and eternally close friendship.

Carla Coté, my very special friend, and a constant source of inspiration.

Sivan Farzan-Coté, my Number One Pal, for showing me that it is all about love and play.

Astrid and Tom Brown, for some heartfelt support when it was really needed.

Dee Eva Black, Leila Nader, Ken Norquay, and Markus Radtke, who attended the first meetings to explore the ideas and the exercises presented in this book, and offered their own valuable insights.

The many wonderful baristas at Delany's Coffee House where I wrote some of the book.

Sharon at TheNewYou.bizz for her help in formatting the cover for the book and converting it to digital format.

Endnotes

[1] Thomas Nagel, *The View From Nowhere*, (New York: Oxford University Press, 1986), p. 55. Emphasis in the original.

[2] Henri Tajfel, "Experiments in Intergroup Discrimination," *Scientific American*, Nov. 1970, p. 96.

[3] *Pascal's Pensées or, Thoughts on Religion*, trans. by Gertrude Burfurd Rawlings, (Mount Vernon, New York: Peter Pauper Press, ND), p. 36.

[4] Swami Muktananda, *Play of Consciousness*, (South Fallsburg, New York: Syda Foundation, 1978), p. 183.

[5] It should be noted that some interpretations are that it is not a merge but the recognition that Atman and Brahman are the same entity. However in normal waking consciousness there is no *perception* that they are the same so whether Samadhi appears as a merging or the recognition of a unity seems moot.

[6] James H. Austin, *Zen and the Brain*, (Cambridge, MA: MIT Press, 1998), p. 303.

[7] Austin, p. 492.

[8] Austin, p. 493.

[9] Austin, p. 303

[10] James H. Austin, *Zen and the Brain*, (Cambridge, MA: MIT Press, 1998), 303.

[11] Austin, p. 555. Emphasis in the original.

[12] Austin, p. 651. Emphasis in the original.

[13] Austin, p. 652. Emphasis in the original.

[14] See for instance Mrithunjay Rathore et al, "Functional Connectivity of Prefrontal Cortex in Various Meditation Techniques—A Mini-Review," *International Review of Yoga*, 15, 2022.

[15] Thanh-Lan Ngo, "Review of the effects of mindfulness meditation on mental and physical health and its mechanisms of action," *Mental Health in Quebec*, 38:2 2013, p. 23.

[16] Austin, p. 416.

[17] Pema Chödrön, "Pema Chödrön on Meditation and the Middle Way," *Lion's Roar*, June 19. 2020.

[18] Sam Keen, "String of Theories." *New York Times Book Review*, March 8, 2015, p. 22.

[19] T.S. Eliot, "Burnt Norton."

[20] David M. Buss, "The Evolution of happiness," *American Psychologist*, Jan. 2000. p. 17.

[21] Buss, p. 17. Emphasis in the original.

22 Antonio Damasio, *The Feeling of What Happens*, (New York: Harcourt Brace & Company, 1999), p. 169.

23 Damasio, p. 125.

24 David Brooks, "How Faith Shapes My Politics," *New York Times*, Sept. 25, 2020.

25 David Hume, *A Treatise of Human Nature*, 1739, (New York: Barnes & Noble, 2005), p. 193.

26 Philip Cushman, "Why the Self is Empty," *American Psychologist*, 45:5, May, 1990, p. 600.

27 Cushman, pp. 600-601.

28 Brandt, p. 92.

29 Vivien Gornick, "Put on the Diamonds," *Harper's*, Oct. 2021.

30 Allan N. Schore, "Early Superego Development: The Emergence of Shame and Narcissistic Affect Regulation in the Practicing Period," *Psychoanalysis and Contemporary Thought*, 14: 2, 1991, 194.

31 James N. Kirby et al, "Human evolution and culture in relationship to shame in the parenting role: Implications for psychology and psychotherapy," *Psychology and Psychotherapy: Theory, Research & Practice*. June 2019. 92: 2, p. 3.

32 Kirby, p. 4

33 Kirby, p. 5.

34 Kirby, p. 6.

35 Kirby, p. 6.

36 Robert Karen, "Shame," *Atlantic Monthly*, Feb. 1992. P. 43-46.

37 Frank Bruni, "The Magic and Moral of Joan Didion," *New York Times*, Nov. 8, 2017.

38 Joey Berlin, *Toxic Fame*, (Detroit: Visible Ink Press, 1996), p. 33.

39 Sue Erikson Bloland, "Fame: The Power and Cost of a Fantasy," *The Atlantic Monthly*, Nov. 1999, p. 60.

40 John A. Bargh and Tanya L. Chartrand, "The Unbearable Automaticity of Being," *American Psychologist*, July, 1999, p. 462.

41 Thanh-Lan Ngo, "Review of the effects of mindfulness meditation on mental and physical health and its mechanisms of action," *Mental Health in Quebec*, 38:2 2013, p. 21.

42 Stephen Cave, "There's no such thing as Free Will," *The Atlantic*, June, 2016, p. 70.

43 Lawrence W. Barsalou, *Cognitive Psychology*, Hillsdale : 1992 Lawrence Erlbaum, p. 91

44 Cave, p. 72.

45 Roy F. Baumeister, "How the Self Became a Problem: A Psychological Review of Historical Research," *J. of Personality and Social Psychology*, 52:1, 1987, p. 170.

46 Jennifer Szalai, "Reality Bites," *NYT Book Review*, Oct. 1, 2023.

47 "shit happens," *Psychology Today*, May/June 1995.

48 Milan Kundera, "Man Thinks, God Laughs," *New York Review of Books*, June 13, 1985.

49 James Austin, *Zen and the* Brain, 416.

50 Milan Kundera, "Man Thinks, God Laughs," *New York Review of Books*, June 13, 1985.

51 Wayne C. Booth, "What do we mean when we talk about irony?" *Harper's*, May, 1984.

52 Scott McLemee, "What Price Utopia." *NYT Book Review*, Nov. 25, 2007.

53 Daniel Gilbert, *Stumbling on Happiness*, Knopf. Reviewed by Scott Stossel, "The Joy of Delusion," *NYT Book Review*, May 7, 2006, p. 16.

54 Niels Bohr, quoted in Otto Frisch, *What Little I Remember*.

55 Bernard Williams, "The Riddle of Umberto Eco," *New York Review of Books*, Feb. 2, 1995.

56 Hans Christian von Baeyer, "In Search of Nothing," *Sciences*, Mar/Apr 1987.

57 Robert Lustig, *The Hacking of the American Mind*, p. 10.

58 Stephen Batchelor, *Buddhism Without Beliefs*, (New York: Riverhead Books, 1997), p. 5.

59 Batchelor, p. 5. Emphasis added.

60 Batchelor, p. 40. Emphasis added.

61 Batchelor, p. 25.

62 Batchelor, p.41.

63 Victor Stenger, James Lindsay, & Peter Boghossian, "Physicists are Philosophers, Too," *Scientific American*, May 8, 2015.

64 Quoted in Otto Frisch, *What Little I Remember*, Cambridge, 1980.

65 Sadri Hassani, "Sources of Quantum Voodooism," *Skeptical Inquirer*, Nov/Dec, 2020, p. 46. Emphasis in the original.

66 Quoted in Hassani, p. 46. Emphasis added.

67 Srdja Popovic and Mladen Joksic, "Why Dictators Don't Like Jokes," *Foreign Policy*, April 5, 2013.

68 Stephen Batchelor, interviewed in *What is Enlightenment?*, Fall/Winter 1998, p.103.

69 T.S. Eliot, "Little Gidding."

70 Friar Allen Kramer, channeling Heraclitus.

9 781068 826108